SOUTH CAROLINA
SPORTS LEGENDS

The University of South Carolina football team is pictured after the "Big Thursday" game in 1912. South Carolina Athletic Hall of Famer Fritz von Kolnitz holds the game ball after the 22-7 Gamecock victory at the South Carolina Fairgrounds on Elmwood Avenue. (Safron Antiques.)

FRONT COVER: Army fullback and 1945 Heisman Trophy winner Doc Blanchard. (West Point.)
COVER BACKGROUND: Newberry College football team. (Newberry College.)
BACK COVER: Furman basketball star Frank Selvy. (Furman University.)

SOUTH CAROLINA
SPORTS LEGENDS

Ernie Trubiano
on behalf of the South Carolina Athletic Hall of Fame

ARCADIA
PUBLISHING

Copyright © 2009 by Ernie Trubiano
ISBN 978-0-7385-6655-9

Published by Arcadia Publishing
Charleston, South Carolina

Printed in the United States of America

Library of Congress Control Number: 2009938725

For all general information contact Arcadia Publishing at:
Telephone 843-853-2070
Fax 843-853-0044
E-mail sales@arcadiapublishing.com
For customer service and orders:
Toll-Free 1-888-313-2665

Visit us on the Internet at www.arcadiapublishing.com

CONTENTS

ACKNOWLEDGMENTS

*The achievements of an organization are the results of the combined effort of
each individual. Individual commitment to a group effort—that is what makes
a team work, a company work, a society work, a civilization work.*

—Vince Lombardi

No help, no book. That's the bottom line.

This book would not have been possible without the support—technical, moral, and otherwise—from others. Thanks, foremost, to the South Carolina Athletic Hall of Fame (SCAHOF), especially executive director Ephraim Ulmer, the glue of the organization, for his encouragement and guidance, and to his administrative assistant Heather Mays for her many contributions.

Digital guru Mike Safran provided untold photographs from his Safran's Antiques vintage collection. College sports information directors—especially SCAHOF board members Andy Solomon of the Citadel and Sam Blackman of Clemson—came through with other information and photographs. Other SCAHOF board members also chipped in with forgotten tidbits, and longtime board members/inductees Dom Fusci and Bill Hudson provided nuggets of wisdom.

My endearing wife, Bootsie, who put up with my keyboard clanging with only a smidgen of whining, sacrificed family time during the project.

Last, but not least, grateful thanks must go to the many inductees and volunteer board members from the past 50 years of the South Carolina Athletic Hall of Fame. Without the likes of Herman Helms, Weems Baskin, and Frank Howard, there would not be a shrine devoted to Palmetto State sports stars. And without determined leadership from past presidents—especially Grant Bennett, who strived to his last breath to see the groundbreaking of a House of Heroes—the South Carolina Athletic Hall of Fame would not have endured.

—Ernie Trubiano
June 1, 2009

The year following each athlete's name denotes the year they were inducted into the South Carolina Athletic Hall of Fame.

ABBREVIATIONS

SCAHOF   South Carolina Athletic Hall
   of Fame
USC   University of South Carolina
NFL   National Football League
AFL   American Football League
NBA   National Basketball Association
PGA   Professional Golfers' Association

LPGA   Ladies Professional Golf Association
NASCAR   National Association of Stock
   Car and Auto Racing
NAIA   National Association of
   Intercollegiate Athletics
SIAA   Southern Intercollegiate
   Athletics Association

INTRODUCTION

The sports page records people's accomplishments; the front page has nothing but man's failures.

—Earl Warren

Despite its relatively small population (4,321,249 in the 2006 census to rank as the 26th most populous state), South Carolina has been blessed with an abundance of sports luminaries as well as a plethora of adoring sports fans.

Within this book, followers of all sports can peruse, in capsule form, the accomplishments of the best stars of the past 50 years. This book is not intended to be a comprehensive history of sports in South Carolina but rather a pictorial snapshot of individual legends who have given South Carolinians precious memories and relief from life's travails.

The South Carolina Athletic Hall of Fame (SCAHOF), formed in the 1950s by the South Carolina Association of Sportswriters, honors outstanding athletic achievement/service and lasting contribution to the cause of sports in the Palmetto State. SCAHOF inducted its first class in 1960 in a private ceremony. The charter members included Rex Enright, Walter Johnson, Banks McFadden, Dode Phillips, Frank Selvy, and Steve Wadiak. Bill Rone of the *State* served as the SCAHOF committee chairman. An old-timers committee, charged with naming "significant contributors to athletics prior to January of 1960," conducted the voting for Johnson, Phillips, and McFadden. The South Carolina Association of Sportswriters—led by Jake Penland of the *State*, USC sports information director Red Canup, Warren Koon of the *Charleston Evening Post*, and Ed McGrath of the *Spartanburg Journal*—voted for modern-era inductees Selvy, Wadiak, and Enright.

After a few years, the organization became dormant but sprang back in 1973 with new vigor and its first public banquet—but with sparse records, especially of years of induction. Herman Helms of the *State* newspaper spearheaded the SCAHOF revival and enlisted the aid of Clemson football coach Frank Howard, University of South Carolina (USC) track coach Weems Baskin, and Les Timms of the Spartanburg *Herald*, with Charles K. Cross as chairman of a 16-member board. Since 1973, the board has elected more than 30 different presidents. Given the constant rotation of presidents and board members, the organization needed continuity, and to this end, in 1997, the hall's leadership named Ephraim Ulmer as its first executive director.

Today the South Carolina Athletic Hall of Fame, through its annual induction banquet, continues the tradition of honoring the state's best sports figures. While still lacking a brick-and-mortar building, the hall is actively striving to build a "House of Heroes" to showcase the collected memorabilia of the more than 260 already-enshrined legends and the many others who will follow them. One day in the near future, sports fans will have a place to visit and view the trophies, uniforms, and other artifacts that accompanied these individuals' journeys to greatness. One day, the South Carolina Athletic Hall of Fame will have a building where the proactive organization will play host to clinics, seminars, and exhibits for aspiring athletes.

To be eligible for the South Carolina Athletic Hall of Fame, an athlete must be retired from competition for a minimum of five years. Golfers and tennis players, whose senior circuits allow them to continue playing longer, are exceptions to this rule, becoming eligible at age 50—retired or not. Coaches and contributors also become eligible at age 50. The annual SCAHOF banquet, which attracts about 40 returning inductees and some 650 fans, comprises the greatest assembly of the state's sport stars under one roof, and its audiences have witnessed many of the toughest former competitors tear up at the podium during their induction ceremonies.

The SCAHOF's native-born inductees hail from all corners of the state: from such tiny towns as Bamberg, Bishopville, Cameron, Hickory Grove, and Timmonsville, as well as the metropolitan centers of Charleston, Columbia, and Greenville.

But not all of the SCAHOF's inductees were born here. The hall also honors nonnative South Carolinians who have made an impact on South Carolina and national sports. This group includes New Yorker and USC basketball coach Frank McGuire as well as Georgia-born Gamecock and Heisman Trophy winner George Rogers.

Several SCAHOF inductees were more than tremendous competitors, such Palmetto State athletes as 1920s track and field star Lucille Godbold, Althea Gibson (who opened racial doors in both tennis and female golf tours), Camden's Larry Doby (the American League's Jackie Robinson), and Willie Jeffries (the first African American coach of a NCAA Division I football team), have served their sports—and society as a whole—by courageously breaking down barriers of gender and race.

Some SCAHOF inductees have contributed as economic visionaries for their sports—such as Bob Colvin and Harold Brasington, whose bold investment in the Darlington International Raceway created one of NASCAR's cornerstones. Cot Campbell introduced America to syndicated Thoroughbred racing ownership in 1969, and Marion duPont Scott established the nation's first $100,000 steeplechase race in 1971.

Pioneers in the SCAHOF include John Heisman, who established a level of gridiron excellence that spawned the famous trophy in 1935; Frank Selvy, who shocked the basketball world by pouring in 100 points in a single game in 1954; Larry Nance, winner of the NBA's inaugural Slam Dunk competition in 1984; Xavier McDaniel, the first to lead the nation in both scoring and rebounding in 1985; and in 1970 Buddy Baker, the first to race a stock car at 200-plus miles per hour on an enclosed course.

If being first does not impress, how about simply being the all-time best—as in legendary Summerville High School coach John McKissick, who won more football games at any level—high school, college, or professional—than anyone in history. Think about that: the best ever, right here in South Carolina.

Of course, sports reach beyond touchdowns and home runs to character and sportsmanship. Ambassadors of the games such as Bobby Richardson, Art Baker, Cally Gault, Fisher DeBerry, Bob McNair, Jeff Davis, Barbara Kennedy-Dixon, and Bob Bradley also grace the inductee rolls of the South Carolina Athletic Hall of Fame.

For more South Carolina sports legends, read on.

TURF TITANS

In life, as in a football game, the principle to follow is: Hit the line hard.

—Teddy Roosevelt

It is no coincidence that football, by far, has more athletes inducted into the South Carolina Athletic Hall of Fame than any other sport. Football seems ingrained in South Carolinians. It starts with rabid high school hotbeds and continues with college teams. Although South Carolina's fall passion has been rewarded by only two national championships (Clemson in 1981 and Furman in 1988) and a handful of near misses (USC in 1984, Furman in 1985 and 2001, and Wofford in 1970), the Palmetto State, nevertheless, has produced its share of marquee performers.

Erskine College's Dode Phillips, a charter member of the South Carolina Athletic Hall of Fame, became the state's first football bona fide star, followed by Clemson All-American Banks McFadden. Steve Wadiak, recognized as USC's first superstar, and George Rogers followed suit, leading the nation in rushing and winning the Heisman Trophy in 1980.

The Palmetto State has turned out a host of additional All-Americans and sent hundreds to the professional ranks. Many of these stars have been inducted in the South Carolina Athletic Hall of Fame and still others into the College Football Hall of Fame (Rogers; the Clemson trio of Banks McFadden, Terry Kinard, and Jeff Davis; and South Carolina State's Donnie Shell); the Pro Football Hall of Fame (Deacon Jones and Harry Carson of South Carolina State, and Charleston native Art Shell); and the Canadian Football League Hall of Fame (USC's Dickie Harris). Many grace the rolls of their college's all-time teams and halls of fame.

TOM ADDISON, 2004. The Lancaster native starred as USC linebacker (1955–1957) and an American Football League All-Star with 16 career interceptions, including five in 1962. Addison served as the first president of the AFL Players Association. (University of South Carolina.)

GARY BARNES, 2005. The Clemson star wide receiver (1959–1961) from Fairfax, Alabama, played in the East-West game and Hula Bowl, and went on to a National Football League (NFL) career (1961–1967), helping Green Bay win the NFL championship in 1962. He is the last player to score in a "Big Thursday" game and the first to score for the Atlanta Falcons. (Clemson University.)

THOMAS "BLACK CAT" BARTON, 1987. The Lancaster native and Clemson football star (1949–1952) made All-American in 1952 and played in the Gator, Orange, and Hula Bowls and in the College All-Star Game. Frank Howard chose him for his 30-year all-time team. He served as the longtime president of Greenville Technical College. (Clemson University.)

JOE "HAWK" BLALOCK, 1969. This Clemson football standout (1939–1941) and the school's first two-time All-American led the Tigers in receiving for three consecutive years, helping his team secure a bid to the 1940 Cotton Bowl. (Clemson University.)

DOC BLANCHARD, 1961. Pictured on the right with Glen Davis (No. 41), Bishopville's bullish fullback and linebacker Felix Anthony "Doc" Blanchard (No. 35) led West Point to national titles in 1944 and 1945, and won the Heisman Trophy and the Maxwell and James E. Sullivan Awards in the latter year. He scored 38 touchdowns in his Army career and served as the Cadets' placekicker and punter. *Time* and *Life* magazines featured Blanchard and Army backfield mate Glenn Davis on their covers in 1945. Hollywood caught the fever as well with the 1947 movie *Spirit of West Point*, starring the pair as themselves. West Point coach Earl "Red" Blaik once said of his star, "Imagine a big bruising fullback who runs 100 yards in 10 seconds flat, who kicks off into the end zone, who punts 50 yards, who can also sweep the flank as well as rip the middle, who catches laterals or forward passes with sure-fingered skill, and who makes his own interference. That's Mr. Blanchard." Blanchard served as a jet pilot in the U.S. Air Force during the Korean and Vietnam Wars, flying 113 combat missions and earning the Distinguished Flying Cross. In his honor, the I-20/U.S. Route 15 interchange near Bishopville is named the Felix "Doc" Blanchard Interchange, and the town erected a statue of him. (West Point.)

JEFF BOSTIC, 1999. The Clemson standout offensive lineman (1977–1979) was named to the all-time Tiger team. The Greensboro, North Carolina, native went on to play in four Super Bowls, winning three with the Redskins (1982, 1987, 1991). ESPN picked the 1983 Pro Bowler for its 40-man roster of greatest Super Bowl players in 2006. (Clemson University.)

JOE BOSTIC, 2010. A two-time All-American and All-ACC in 1977 and 1978, Bostic won the Jacobs Blocking Trophy in 1977. He later played offensive guard for the NFL St. Louis Cardinals. Bostic was selected as a member of the 50-year All-ACC team. (Clemson University.)

CHARLIE BRADSHAW, 1980. The Wofford quarterback earned All-State honors three times and gained Little All-American laurels in 1957 before he went on to star in the business world. As cofounder of Spartan Foods and Hardees hamburger franchises. (Wofford College.)

CHARLIE BROWN, 2004. This Johns Island native set South Carolina State and Mid-Eastern Atlantic Conference receiving (26.7 yards per catch) and return records before becoming a two-time NFL Pro Bowl receiver (1982–1983). In his NFL career, Brown had 220 receptions for 3,548 yards (16.1 average) and 25 touchdowns, and played a key role in the Redskins' Super Bowl 1983 and 1984 championship teams. (Washington Redskins.)

BOBBY BRYANT, 1982. The USC football and baseball star (1964–1967) was named All-ACC in both sports, as well as ACC Athlete of Year. Bryant was a stellar defensive back and kick returner (setting a school record with a 98-yard punt return) and a southpaw pitcher who set the school record for career strikeouts. Nicknamed "Bones" for his wiry 6-foot, 175-pound frame, Bryant enjoyed a great NFL career (1967–1981) with the Minnesota Vikings, playing in the Pro Bowl and four Super Bowls. He made All-Pro in 1975 and picked off 57 career interceptions. The Macon, Georgia, native is also a member of the George Hall of Fame. (University of South Carolina.)

JEFF BRYANT, 2004. The Clemson second-team All-American played a key role on the Tigers' 1981 national championship team, leading the Tigers in sacks and tackles for losses. The defensive lineman from Atlanta became a first-round draft pick, number six overall, and went on to set sack records (with a career high of 14.5 in 1984) in an 11-year career with the NFL Seattle Seahawks. In 1996, he was named to Clemson's All-Centennial team. (Clemson University.)

JERRY BUTLER, 1997. After earning 14 letters in four sports at Ware Shoals High School, Butler became a first-team Clemson All-America wide receiver in 1978 and MVP of the 1977 Gator Bowl. The first-round NFL pick had 139 career catches for 2,223 yards and 11 touchdowns and played eight years of professional ball, setting one-game records of 255 yards and four touchdowns for the Buffalo Bills. He twice won the Bills' "Man of the Year" for his community service. He is a member of Clemson's Ring of Honor. (Clemson University.)

MARION CAMPBELL, 1984. The Chester native became an All-American lineman and three-time All-SEC star at the University of Georgia. After an NFL career in which he made All-Pro in 1960, he served as head coach of the Philadelphia Eagles and Atlanta Falcons. (Philadelphia Eagles.)

JOHN CANNADY, 1991. The Charleston native became an All-Big 10 linebacker at Indiana (1945–1947) and a Pro Bowl selection (1950) and All-Pro (1951, 1953) with the New York Giants. He was voted the NFL's most outstanding player in 1950. (New York Giants.)

JAMES C. "J. C." CAROLINE, 1976. The four-sport star at Columbia's Booker T. Washington High School became a football All-American at Illinois (1953–1954), where he led the nation in rushing with 1,256 yards. He went on to a stellar NFL career with the Chicago Bears (1956–1963), with 24 career interceptions and an All-Pro appearance in 1956. He is also a member of the College Football Hall of Fame. (University of Illinois.)

HARRY CARSON, 1989. The Florence native blossomed into a two-time All-State and two-time All-Mid-Eastern Atlantic Conference star, and an AP Small College All-American at South Carolina State in 1975—as well as being elected senior class president. He then became a Pro-Bowl linebacker, defensive captain, and Super Bowl champion (1987) during a 14-year career with the New York Giants—a career that catapulted him into the Pro Football Hall of Fame in 2006. Carson made 19 career sacks and 11 interceptions. He made the College Hall of Fame in 2002. (South Carolina State University.)

BARNEY CHAVOUS, 1992. The Aiken native and All-American (1971–1973) became the NFL defensive rookie of the year in 1974 and played defensive end and tackle for the Denver Broncos through 1986. He held the team sack record when he retired. He made the Pro-Bowl and All-Pro in his 14-year career, and worked tirelessly for charities. He is a member of the Aiken, Mid-Eastern Atlantic Conference, and South Carolina State Halls of fame. (South Carolina State University.)

DWIGHT CLARK, 1986. The unheralded Clemson end (1975–1978) averaged 17.3 yards per catch during college career and developed into a fine NFL receiver at San Francisco, where he will forever be known for "the Catch" from 49ers' quarterback Joe Montana. He twice made the Pro Bowl, and in 1982, he made All-Pro and NFL Player of the Year by *Sports Illustrated*. (Clemson University.)

DWIGHT CLARK

EARL CLARY, 1968. He earned the nickname "the Gaffney Ghost" while starring as an elusive ball carrier at USC (1931–1933). The 1933 All-Southern selection led the Gamecocks to three consecutive victories over Clemson. (University of South Carolina.)

JAMES HARTLEY COLEMAN, 1989. The three-sport star at Florence High School became Furman's football captain and All-State center (1921–1924). He later coached Honea Path High School from 1925 to 1939 and again from 1942 to 1946, compiling a 101-56-17 record and winning state championships in 1937 and 1945. After coaching, he officiated football games in high school and college while serving as a school administrator. (Furman University.)

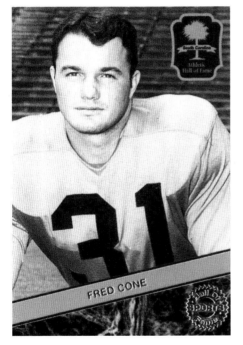

FRED CONE, 1973. The Clemson walk-on who did not play high school football became the Tigers' first 2,000-yard rusher (1948–1950), scored 31 touchdowns, and starred on two undefeated teams before playing in the NFL from 1951 to 1957 with the Green Bay Packers. At Green Bay. The Pine Apple, Alabama, native would score 455 points on 16 touchdowns, 53 field goals, and 200 points after touchdowns. Clemson coach Frank Howard described Cone as, "the best player I ever coached." Cone is a member of the Clemson Ring of Honor. (Clemson University.)

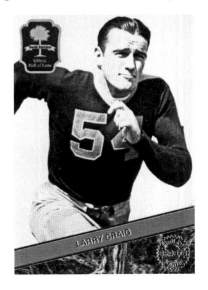

LARRY CRAIG, 1975. Craig was an All-Southern Conference end in 1938 at USC, where he served as captain of the football and track teams. He became a six-time two-way NFL All-Pro as a blocking back-defensive end with Green Bay from 1939 to 1950. He is a member of the Green Bay Packers Hall of Fame. (University of South Carolina.)

BENNIE CUNNINGHAM, 1993. The Seneca All-State star continued his football success at nearby Clemson, catching 64 passes for 1,044 yards and 10 touchdowns. The All-ACC star and two-time All-American (1974–1975) became a first-round pick in 1976 and a standout NFL tight end for Pittsburgh (1976–1985), helping the Steelers win Super Bowls in 1978 and 1979. (Clemson University.)

BILL CURRIER, 2010. As a USC senior in 1976, Currier won awards as team MVP, highest academics, and captain—the only player to win all in one season. The Glen Burnie, Maryland, native made the Blue-Gray All-Star Game and went on to play nine years in the NFL as a defensive back with the Houston Oilers (as an All-Rookie team pick), New England, and his final five with the New York Giants. While there, he won the New York City Touchdown Club Unsung Hero Award for community involvement. (University of South Carolina.)

JIM DAVID, 1994. Born in Florence and raised in North Charleston, David played in two College World Series and ranked second in the nation in pass receiving at Colorado A&M before becoming a six-time Pro Bowler (1955–1960) for the NFL Detroit Lions. He made All-Pro cornerback in 1954 and helped lead the Lions to three world championships and four division titles. He later served as an NFL assistant coach for 13 years. The Lions named him to their all-time team in 2008. (Detroit Lions.)

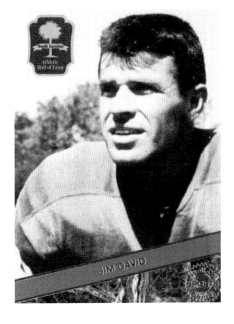

JEFF DAVIS, 2001. The Clemson star (1978–1981) made ACC Player of the Year and first-team All-American linebacker as a senior when he led the team in tackles with 175. The team captain led the 12-0 Tigers to the national championship in 1981, and Davis was named MVP of the Orange Bowl. The Greensboro, North Carolina, native is a member of the College Football Hall of Fame and the Clemson Ring of Honor. (Clemson University.)

SAM DAVIS, 1991. An Allen University star of 1960s from Ocilla, Georgia, Davis became a stalwart offensive lineman and team captain for Pittsburgh, helping the Steelers win four Super Bowls. (Pittsburgh Steelers.)

SAM DELUCA, 2002. A USC lineman (1954–1956), Jacobs Blocking Trophy winner, and third-team All-American as a senior, Deluca played in the College All-Star Game and Senior Bowl. The Brooklyn, New York, native then went on to star in the CFL for three seasons and for the AFL San Diego Chargers for three years before becoming captain and stalwart blocker for Joe Namath with the New York Jets for four years. He later became a broadcaster with CBS. (University of South Carolina.)

KING DIXON, 1977. Dixon was a Laurens native and star all-purpose running back, defensive back, and punter for USC (1956–1958). In 1957, he returned the opening kickoff in two consecutive games—98 yards against Texas, and 89 yards against Furman. He played and coached with the Quantico Marines team and won the Armed Services Outstanding Athlete award after winning three medals in Vietnam. He later served as USC's athletics director. (University of South Carolina.)

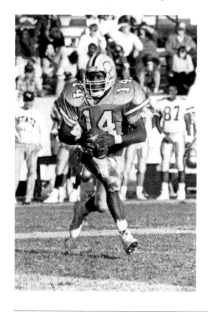

JACK DOUGLAS, 2007. The Citadel star finished his career as all-time leading rushing quarterback in Division 1-AA. He led the Bulldogs to a Southern Conference championship and a tie for No. 1 in the final Division 1-AA poll in 1992. During his career, the two-time team captain engineered upsets over Davy, USC, Arkansas, and Army twice. The Citadel retired his jersey in 1993. (Citadel.)

STEVE FULLER, 1991. The star quarterback at Spartanburg High School became a two-time ACC Player of the Year and two-time Academic All-American at Clemson. He played in the NFL (1975–1978) for the Chiefs and Bears. His alma mater retired his jersey and inducted him into the Clemson Ring of Honor. (Clemson University.)

DOM FUSCI, 1991. Two-time All-Southern Conference (1942–1943) stud lineman at South Carolina, Fusci (No. 43) played in the College-Pro All-Star Game and became a two-way All Pro in the AFL in 1948. The native New Yorker later reigned as a four-time South Carolina Handball Doubles champion and served for 22 years as a high school and college sports official. "Dynamite Dom," chosen for the all-time first-half century Gamecock team during USC's centennial celebration in 1995, also served above and beyond the call of duty as a SCAHOF past president and a longtime board member. (University of South Carolina.)

BOBBY GAGE, 1978. The Anderson native and All-American all-purpose back for Clemson (1945–1948), Gage led the Tigers' unbeaten 1948 team and later played for the NFL's Pittsburgh Steelers. (Clemson University.)

BILLY GAMBRELL, 1995. A football and track star at USC (1959–1962), Gambrell twice made All-ACC (1961–1962). In football, he compiled 2,300 all-purpose yards over three seasons. In track, he recorded a 23-foot-plus broad jump. The Athens, Georgia, native later went on to play 12 seasons as an NFL wide receiver. (University of South Carolina.)

DREHER GASKIN, 2004. A three-sport standout at Clemson and later for the Armed Forces Team in 1955–1956, the 6-foot, 4-inch; 230-pound All-ACC end played in the Blue-Gray Game. (Clemson University.)

JOHN GILLIAM, 1992. The Greenwood-born South Carolina State star receiver of the 1960s later led the NFL in average yards per catch in 1970 and 1971. For his 10-year NFL career while playing for five teams, Gilliam caught 382 passes for 7,056 yards (18.5 average) and 48 touchdowns, and averaged 25.5 yards on kickoff returns. He made All-Pro once and played in the Pro Bowl three times. (New Orleans Saints.)

SANDY GILLIAM, 1989. A three-sport star at Lancaster Sims High School in late 1940s and at Allen University in early 1950s, Gilliam later compiled a 235-23 overall high school coaching record at Sims High School and Barr Street High School (1953–1964) and a 91-18-1 mark at Maryland State (1964–1968). (Maryland State.)

BUDDY GORE, 2000. The Conway native and Clemson star (1965–1967) became the Tigers' first 1,000-yard rusher and earned the ACC Player of Year honor in 1966. (Clemson University.)

JEFF GRANTZ, 1988. The football and baseball standout (1973–1976) ranks among the best two-sport athletes in USC history. A quarterback proficient in passing and running, Grantz rates high in every school passing category and earned second-team All-American in 1975. In baseball, he set a Gamecock fielding record as a middle infielder. (University of South Carolina.)

HAROLD GREEN, 2006. A two-time All-South star at USC (1986–1989), Green led the Gamecocks in rushing three times. He enjoyed an eight-year NFL career, making the 1990 Pro Bowl when he rushed for 1,170 yards for Cincinnati. He finished his career with Atlanta in the Super Bowl. (University of South Carolina.)

ART GREGORY, 1983. Aiken native Gregory became a two-time Duke All-American lineman (1962–1963), both times winning the Jacobs Blocking Trophy while leading the Blue Devils to three ACC titles. The two-way performer is a member of the Duke All-Time team. (Duke University.)

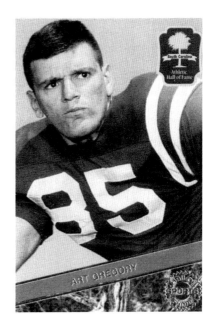

TATUM GRESSETTE, 1979. A beloved Palmetto State athlete who starred in football for two years at Furman (1917–1918) and two years at USC (1920–1921), he later served as coach-AD at the Citadel. Gressette also officiated major college football games for 22 years, including many bowl games and the College All-Star Game. The St. Matthews native is a member of all three schools' halls of fame, as well as the South Carolina Golf Hall of Fame. (University of South Carolina.)

DICKIE HARRIS, 2001. An All-ACC and All-American from Point Pleasant, New Jersey, Harris was a versatile defensive back, running back, and return specialist at USC (1969–1971). He made the long return his trademark–nine times making runbacks of 50 yards or more. He went on to become a seven-time Canadian Football League All-Star with the Montreal Alouettes and is enshrined in the Canadian Football League Hall of Fame (University of South Carolina.)

ALEX HAWKINS, 1979. The USC football star (1956–1958) earned ACC Player of the Year and third-team All-American in 1958 and later became a versatile NFL standout. Hawkins, from Welch, West Virginia, played for Baltimore (1959–1965 and again in 1967) and for Atlanta (1966), where he enjoyed his best season, with 44 receptions. Nicknamed "Captain Who" when he became the NFL's first special teams captain with the Colts, he helped Baltimore to championship games in 1956 and 1966. (University of South Carolina.)

BOB HUDSON, 1985. The North Charleston native and Clemson football and track star (1948–1950) displayed a rare blend of speed and power in track and field while competing in the 100, 220, discus and shot put. The All-State and All Southern star played 11 years as a professional linebacker in both the NFL and AFL, three times making All-NFL second team. He set a league record of 11 interceptions in 1954. (Clemson University.)

BILL HUDSON, 1979. An All-State star in three sports at North Charleston, he ranks as one of the greatest linemen at Clemson (1954–1956). He made first-team All-Canadian Football League in 1959 and 1960 with Montreal, and then made All-American Football League while helping lead the San Diego Chargers to a championship. The burly offensive lineman served as the Chargers team captain in 1962 and 1963. Hudson has been a key SCAHOF board member. (Clemson University.)

B. C. INABINET, 1986. The hefty star Clemson football lineman (1953–1955) went on to play in the Canadian Football League. (Clemson University.)

ERNIE JACKSON, 2008. A Columbia native, Jackson starred at Lower Richland High School and became a two-time All-American at Duke, the 1971 ACC Player of the Year, and a member of the ACC Silver Anniversary team and the all-time Duke team. He played nine years in the NFL (intercepting nine passes) with New Orleans, Atlanta, and Detroit. (Duke University.)

LARKIN JENNINGS, 1981. A Bishopville native and star quarterback-halfback at the Citadel (1930–1932), Jennings twice made All-State and All-Southern Conference. (Citadel.)

STANFORD JENNINGS, 2006. The Summerville All-State star helped Furman win four Southern Conference titles while earning league Player of Year honors three times and third-team All-American as a senior in 1984. He played in the Blue-Gray and Senior Bowls before moving on to an NFL career. Furman University has retired his No. 27. (Furman University.)

BOB JONES, 1976. A Clemson athlete (1927–1930), Jones played basketball and football, and served as an assistant football coach. The native of Starr earned the nickname "the General" after a long military stint. He also coached the Clemson boxing team for 12 years, winning two Southern Conference titles. (Clemson University.)

David "Deacon" Jones, 1980. A South Carolina State star defensive end, Jones embarked on an 11-year NFL career as the leader of Los Angeles Rams' "Fearsome Foursome," which earned him induction into the Pro Football Hall of Fame. The two-time NFL Defensive Player of the Year (1968–1969) from Eatonville, Florida, made eight Pro Bowl appearances. He also introduced the head-slap defensive technique, coined the term "sack," and made that big defensive play his trademark with 180.5 career sacks, including 26 in 1967 and 24 in 1968. (Los Angeles Rams.)

Terry Kinard, 2002. The CBS 1982 Defensive Player of the Year and two-time All-American defensive back at Clemson—the only unanimous selection in school history—Kinard helped the Tigers win a national championship in 1981. The former Sumter star became a standout NFL performer (1982–1990), winning the 1986 Super Bowl with the New York Giants. *USA-Today* named him to its 1980s All-Decade team and *Sports Illustrated* named him to its All-Century team. He is a member of the College Football Hall of Fame and the Clemson Ring of Honor. (Clemson University.)

BOB KING, 1973. An All-Southern Conference and All-American football star at Furman (1934–1936), King also excelled in track. The Ranger, Texas, native coached the Paladins' football team for 15 years (1958–1972) with a 60-88-4 record. (Furman University.)

LEVON KIRKLAND, 2008. Lamar native and first-team All-American linebacker at Clemson, Kirkland led the Tigers' No. 1–ranked defense in 1990 and 1991. The Mazda Gator Bowl MVP became a two-time All-Pro with the NFL Steelers in 1996 and 1997, and played in Super Bowl XXX. He was named to Clemson's All-Centennial team in 1996. (Clemson University.)

KEVIN LONG, 2003. A great power runner for USC (1974–1976), Long led the Gamecocks in rushing in 1975 with 1,133 yards. The Clinton star went on to a stellar NFL career with the New York Jets (1977–1981) and then three years in the United States Football League (USFL). (University of South Carolina.)

PAUL MAGUIRE, 1986. Named the Southern Conference Player of Year as a receiver, defensive end, and punter at the Citadel in 1957 and third-team All-American 1959, Maguire holds a school record 83-yard punt. The Youngstown, Ohio, native punted for 11 years in the AFL with the Chargers and Bills before becoming a broadcaster for NBC and ESPN. (Citadel.)

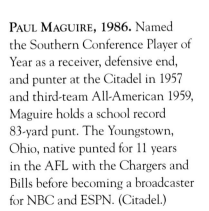

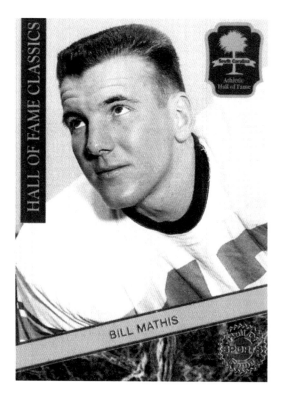

BILL MATHIS, 1977. An outstanding running back at Clemson (1957–1959), the Rocky Mount, North Carolina, native enjoyed an AFL All-Star career with the New York Titans and Jets. Mathis earned an All-Pro laurel once and Pro Bowl honors three times. The Jets named Mathis team MVP in 1962, and he helped the Jets win the 1969 Super Bowl—a victory that helped hasten the AFL-NFL merger. (Clemson University.)

BANKS MCFADDEN, 1960. The Clemson star (1937–1939) was recognized as the Tigers' all-time greatest athlete, made All-American in football and basketball, and had both jerseys retired. In 1939, the Associated Press named him "America's most versatile athlete." He played one season of pro football before an off-season car crash ended his career. The Great Falls native also starred in five track events. The College Football Hall of Fame inducted him in 1959. McFadden is a charter member of the South Carolina Athletic Hall of Fame. (Clemson University.)

STUMP MITCHELL, 1999. A star running back at the Citadel, Mitchell averaged 149.7 yards and ranked No. 3 in the nation in 1980 with a single-season school-record 1,647 yards to become the Bulldogs career rushing leader with 4,062 yards. The 1980 Southern Conference Player of the Year from St. Mary's, Georgia, had his No. 35 jersey retired and went on to become a standout NFL rusher-return man and then a college and professional coach. (Citadel.)

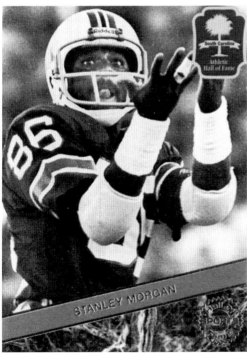

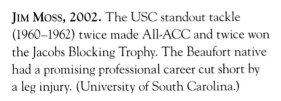

STANLEY MORGAN, 1994. The speedy wide receiver starred at Easley, Tennessee, and in the NFL with the New England Patriots, where he averaged 19.2 yards per catch and amassed more than 10,000 yards in receptions. (New England Patriots.)

JIM MOSS, 2002. The USC standout tackle (1960–1962) twice made All-ACC and twice won the Jacobs Blocking Trophy. The Beaufort native had a promising professional career cut short by a leg injury. (University of South Carolina.)

HARRY OLSZEWSKI, 1990. Olszewski, from Baltimore, was a first-team consensus All-American guard at Clemson in 1967 and won the Jacobs Blocking Trophy. (Clemson University.)

JIMMY ORR, 1978. A Seneca native and All-SEC wide receiver at Georgia, Orr led the league in receiving in 1955 and 1957. He earned the NFL Rookie of the Year honor in 1958, twice won Pro Bowl laurels, and made All-NFL in 1959. He caught 400 passes for 66 touchdowns and 7,920 yards (19.8 yards per catch) in his 13-year NFL career with the Steelers and Colts. He played in two Super Bowls with the Colts and helped the team win the title in 1970. (University of Georgia.)

MICHAEL DEAN PERRY, 2005, AND WILLIAM "REFRIGERATOR" PERRY, 2005. First-team All-ACC and All-American defensive end at Clemson in 1987, Michael Perry (like his brother, born in Aiken) became a six-time NFL Pro-Bowler and four-time All-Pro with the Cleveland Browns. He was named a member of the Tigers' All-Centennial team in 1996. William Perry starred as a middle guard on Clemson's 1981 national championship team. Nicknamed "the Refrigerator" because of his massive, heavy build, Perry became a media sensation, playing in Superbowl XX for the NFL Chicago Bears, in which the erstwhile defensive lineman was given the ball, scoring a touchdown (Clemson University.)

DODE PHILLIPS, 1960. The great athlete and coach at Erskine College starred in baseball and as a single-wing tailback in football (1917–1921). He turned down a professional football contract because he did not want to play on Sundays. He was a charter member of the SCAHOF. In 1950, sportswriters named him best athlete of the first half of the 20th century in South Carolina. So great was Phillips's fame that, when he died in 1965, the *State* newspaper carried his obituary on the front page. (Erskine College.)

ROBERT PORCHER, 2009. The Wando native dominated as a South Carolina State senior with 88 tackles, 15 sacks (two shy of Pro Football Hall of Fame member Harry Carson's school record) and 24 tackles for losses to become a first-round draft pick of the NFL Detroit Lions. The 6-foot, 3-inch; 266-pound defensive end led the Lions in sacks eight times and played in the Pro Bowl three times. South Carolina State retired his No. 94 jersey in 2000. He founded the Detroit Football Classic to benefit college scholarships. (South Carolina State University.)

DEWEY PROCTOR, 1984. The Furman football and baseball great later played professionally as a triple-threat back. The Lake View native made All-State in 1940, 1941, and 1942. In 1942, he also made All-Southern Conference, earned MVP honors in the Carolina Bowl, and played in the Blue-Gray Game. After spending 1943 in the service, he played three years for the New York Yankees football team as a two-way starter in 1948 and did the same for the Chicago Rockets in 1949. He is on Furman's all-time team. He served as the longtime chief of police in Mullins. (Furman University.)

GRADY RAY, 1999. As a baseball and football standout at Newberry College (1952–1956), Ray led the Indians in rushing and receiving, and made the All-Little Four first team. He led the state of South Carolina in rushing in 1953. As a second baseman, he led Newberry in stolen bases twice. The Camden native became a college football referee for 31 years, calling several major bowls. (Newberry College.)

DAN REEVES, 1976. The former USC quarterback (1962–1964) from Americus, Georgia, helped the Dallas Cowboys win the 1971 Super Bowl as a running back and then became an outstanding NFL head coach with a 201-174-2 record, making him the seventh-winningest NFL coach of all time. At USC he played like a coach on the field, and at Dallas he actually served as a player-coach during the final three seasons of his eight-year Cowboys career. He took Denver to the AFC title and the Super Bowl three times (1986, 1987, 1989) and Atlanta once (1998). (University of South Carolina.)

JAMES "LEE" RHAME, 1980. Furman's halfback from 1917 to 1921, Rhame led the 1920 team that outscored foes 286-16 and compiled a 9-1 record. The Holly Hill native played every minute of every game at Furman and made All-State three times. He starred in college and semiprofessional baseball before becoming Florence High School's coach, where his basketball and baseball teams went on to win state titles, and he coached the South Carolina team to a Shrine Bowl victory in football. (Furman University.)

JERRY RICHARDSON, 1975. A two-time National Association of Intercollegiate Athletics (NAIA) and Little All-American at Wofford, Richardson led all South Carolina colleges in scoring three times, averaging 19 yards per catch. Though only a 13th-round pick by the Baltimore Colts in 1958, he went on to finish third in the NFL balloting for Rookie of Year. In his second season, the Spring Hope, North Carolina, native caught eight passes for 90 yards and a touchdown in the NFL championship game. He used the $4,864 in playoff money to buy a hamburger restaurant with former Wofford teammate Charlie Bradshaw, which the two eventually built into the Hardees national franchise, which, along with other food acquisitions, they sold in 1989 for $1.65 billion. Richardson used the money to become the first former NFL player to own an NFL team when he founded the Carolina Panthers in 1993. (Wofford College.)

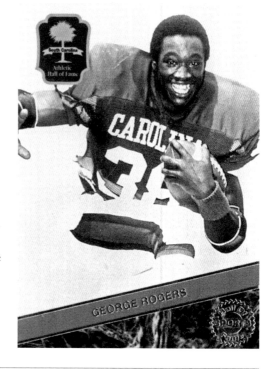

GEORGE ROGERS, 1981. The bruising USC tailback (1977–1980) made consensus All-American and led the nation in rushing with 1,781 yards to win the 1980 Heisman Trophy and Gator Bowl MVP. As a rookie, he led the NFL in rushing, and rushed for more than 1,000 yards in four of his seven professional seasons. The Duluth, Georgia, native is a member of the College Football Hall of Fame. (University of South Carolina.)

BRIAN RUFF, 2006. First-team consensus All-American linebacker at the Citadel in 1976 and Southern Conference and South Carolina Player of Year in 1975 and 1976, Ruff was the first Citadel athlete in history to have his jersey retired. (Citadel.)

MAX RUNAGER, 2007. The USC punter (1976–1979) spent 11 years in the NFL, punting in two Super Bowl victories with the 49ers. Runager, a former Orangeburg star, punted for a 40.2-yard professional average and was named to the Philadelphia Eagles' all-decade team of the 1980s. He was also named to USC's all-time modern era team. (University of South Carolina.)

RICK SANFORD, 1998. The stellar USC defensive back from Rock Hill (1975–1978) earned All-American status as a senior and was selected in the first round by the New England Patriots. He played for seven years in the NFL. (University of South Carolina.)

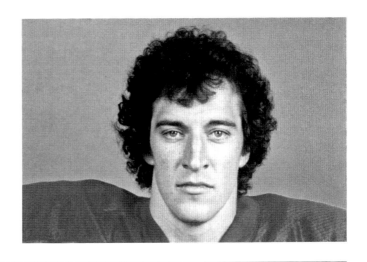

DAVID MARSHALL BARADBURY "JUNE" SCOTT, 1986. In the years 1935–1937, the native of Lake View excelled in football and baseball at Furman, twice making All-Southern Conference in football. The triple-threat quarterback earned the nickname "The Hummingbird" for his elusive quickness. (Furman University.)

WILLIE SCOTT, 2004. The standout tight end from Newberry starred at USC from 1977 to 1980. The first round draft pick by Kansas City in 1981, Scott played six years for the Chiefs and three more with New England Patriots; for a career total of 89 catches for 766 yards, and 15 touchdowns. He was named to USC's all-time roster. (University of South Carolina.)

BOB "RED" SHARPE, 1985. Clemson's center and linebacker (1938–1940) made All-Southern Conference in 1940. The Abbeville native led the Tigers to the Cotton Bowl that year. (Clemson University.)

STERLING SHARPE, 2001. USC's record-setting wide receiver from Glennville, Georgia, made All-American twice (1986 and 1987). He went on to be named All-Pro five times while playing for the Green Bay Packers from 1988 to 1994. He twice led the NFL in receptions, setting records both times and becoming the first player to make 500 catches prior to his seventh season. A 1994 neck injury ended his career prematurely. (Gree Bay Packers.)

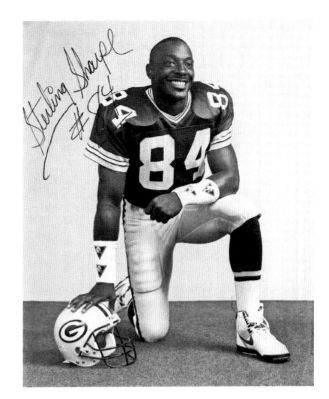

ART SHELL, 1989. The Charleston native and former Bonds-Wilson High School standout went on to become a two-time All-American offensive lineman at Maryland-Eastern Shore, and then starred for 13 years with Oakland Raiders (1968–1982), winning two Super Bowls. Shell made All-Pro four times (1973, 1974, 1976, 1977), and the Pro Bowl eight times. When he became the team's head coach in 1989, 4Shell became the NFL's first African American head coach in the modern era. He is a member of Pro Football Hall of Fame. (Oakland Raiders.)

DONNIE SHELL, 1986. The Whitmire native starred at South Carolina State (1970–1973) where he became an All-America before a standout 11-year NFL career as a three-time All-Pro, five-time Pro Bowler and four-time Super Bowl champion during the Pittsburgh Steelers dynasty years. He retired as the NFL's all-time strong safety interceptions leader with 51. The two-time All-Mid-Eastern Atlantic Conference star is a member of the Black College 100-year Anniversary squad, the National College Football Foundation Hall of Fame, Steelers all-time team, and NFL Silver Anniversary Super Bowl team. (Pittsburgh Steelers.)

RHOTEN SHETLEY, 1981. A stellar two-way back at Furman (1936–1940), Shetley garnered All-South and *Liberty* magazine All-American honors. The Wolf Creek, Tennessee, native played four years of professional football. (Furman University.)

JOHN SMALL, 1988. Small came from Augusta, Georgia, and went on to become Southern Conference Player of the Year and first-team All-American linebacker at the Citadel in 1969. He also made all conference in 1967 and 1968 before playing five years in the NFL—three in Atlanta and two in Detroit. (Citadel Military College.)

FREDDIE SOLOMON, 1993. The elusive 5-foot-11-inch, 184-pound Sumter native ranks as one, if not the best, high school football star in state history. The elusive quarterback ran for more than 500 yards combined in two postseason high school all-star games. He starred at Tampa University and for 11 years as an NFL receiver-returner with the Dolphins (1975–1977) and the 49ers (1978–1985), playing in the 1980 Pro Bowl and the Super Bowl. He caught a career total of 371 passes for 5,846 yards and 48 touchdowns, and rushed for 515 yards. (San Francisco 49ers.)

LOU SOSSAMAN, 1974. The USC center (1940–1942) captained the Gamecocks and became a two-time All-Southern (1941 and 1942), and second-team All-American (1942). He played two years of professional football with the New York Yankees of the AAFC (1946–1948), served with the Navy in World War II. He became the publisher of his hometown newspaper, the *Gaffney Ledger*, and later served on the USC Board of Trustees. (University of South Carolina.)

JAMES HARREL "SPEEDY" SPEER, 1974. The three-sport athlete at Furman (1916–1921) starred at halfback on the 1920 team that outscored opponents 286-16 and went 9-1. The Winston-Salem native made All-State four times and All Southern Conference once. He served in World War I in 1918. He later coached for Greenville High School from 1928 to 1949. (Furman University.)

JIM STUCKEY, 1995. The Cayce-born Stuckey starred at Clemson from 1976 to 1979. The All-American defensive lineman went on to play seven years in the NFL, winning Super Bowl titles with the 49ers in 1982 and 1985. (Clemson University.)

TOMMY SUGGS, 1983. The four-sport star at Lamar High School played at USC from 1968 to 1970 and, despite standing just five-foot-nine-inches, became one of all-time great Gamecock quarterbacks, leading USC to an ACC championship in 1969, defeating Clemson four years in a row, and making Blue-Gray Game MVP. He has since served as the longtime Gamecock radio color analyst. At Suggs' suggestion, Carolina adopted the theme from *2001: A Space Odyssey* for its pre-game entrance-to-the-field music, and it quickly became one of the best introductions in the nation. Suggs has served as president of the South Carolina Athletic Hall of Fame. (University of South Carolina.)

BILLY THOMPSON, 2002. The Greenville-born Maryland State standout made NAIA All-American and went on to be team captain and a two-time All-NFL and three-time Pro-Bowl star in a 13-year NFL career with Denver (1969–1981). He played in Super Bowl XII and is in the Broncos Ring of Fame. (Denver Broncos.)

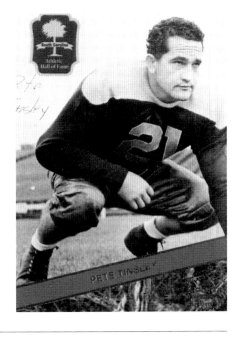

PETE TINSLEY, 1982. The Spartanburg native starred at Spartanburg High School and University of Georgia as lineman and blocking back in the 1930s one-platoon system, and in the NFL for Green Bay (1938–1944). He helped the Packers win two NFL championships and is a member of the Green Bay Packers Hall of Fame. (Green Bay Packers.)

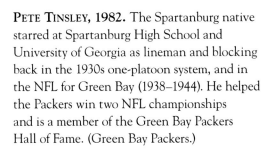

PERRY TUTTLE, 2003. An All-American wide receiver for Clemson's 1981 national championship team, Tuttle was named to Clemson's All-Centennial team in 1996. He is the only Clemson athlete to make the cover of *Sports Illustrated*, in a photograph depicting his touchdown catch. The Lexington, North Carolina, star caught 150 passes for 2,534 yards. (Clemson University.)

STEVE WADIAK, 1960. The two-time All-Southern Conference running back (1950,1951) rushed for 2,878 yards from 1948 to 1951 and played in the Senior and Blue-Gray Bowls. "Wadiak the Cadillac" became USC's first sports superstar, and the first Gamecock athlete to have his jersey retired. Called by his coach Rex Enright "the greatest player I ever coached," the charismatic Wadiak from Chicago died in a 1952 auto accident near Aiken. He is a charter member of the South Carolina Athletic Hall of Fame. (University of South Carolina.)

BOB WATERS, 1987. The Georgia-born Presbyterian College quarterback led Blue Hose to the 1960 Tangerine Bowl where he earned MVP honors. He then defied small-college odds to become an NFL quarterback and defensive back with the 49ers from 1960 to 1964 before turning to coaching. After serving as an assistant at his alma mater, and then Stanford University, Waters became head coach at Western Carolina (1969–1988), earning the NAIA coach-of-the-year honor in 1969. His 1983 Catamounts lost in the NCAA Division 1-AA title game. He compiled a 111-78-6 record in 18 seasons at WCU before succumbing to Amyotrophic lateral sclerosis. (Western Carolina University.)

CHARLIE WATERS, 1980. The North Augusta High School graduate and Clemson defensive back developed into a two-time All-Pro (1977–1978), and three-time Pro Bowl (1976–1978) star with Dallas, and helped win Super Bowls in 1971 and 1977. He was named to the all-time Cowboys team. (Clemson University.)

GEORGE WEBSTER, 1979. The Anderson native and consensus All-America "roverback" at Michigan State in 1965 and 1966, Webster switched to linebacker and made AFL Rookie of Year in 1967 with the Houston Oilers. A three-time winner of All-AFL laurels, Webster was named to the all-time AFL team in 1970 by a panel of veteran football writers. (Michigan State University.)

JOHNNY WEEKS, 1961. A football, basketball, and baseball star at the Citadel (1913–1916), Weeks captained the baseball and football teams. On the latter, Weeks was twice named an All-State quarterback. (Citadel.)

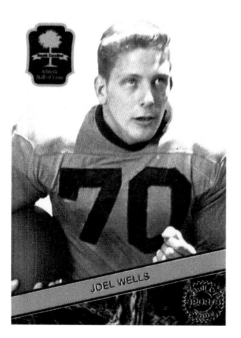

JOEL WELLS, 1974. The two-time All-ACC star at Clemson (1955 and 1956) also made second-team All-American in 1956. The Columbia native played running back for the Montreal Alouettes (1957–1959) and played for the New York Giants 1961 Eastern Division championship team. (Clemson University.)

TURF TITANS

JOHNNIE RICHARD "J. R." WILBURN, 2003.
An all-ACC performer in football and track
for USC in 1965, Wilburn became a standout
NFL receiver with Pittsburgh (1966–1970),
making 123 career catches for 1,834 yards
and eight touchdowns. The Portsmouth,
Virginia, high school star led the Gamecocks
in receiving as a senior with 21 catches for
236 yards. (University of South Carolina.)

JIM YOUNGBLOOD, 1984. The
outstanding all-around athlete at
Jonesville High School became a
two-time All-American linebacker at
Tennessee Tech and played in the Hula
Bowl and College All-Star Game and
Coaches All-American Game. He led
the NFL's Los Angeles Rams in tackles
five times while the team won seven
division titles from 1973 to 1979. The
1979 team won the NFC championship,
losing to Pittsburgh in the Super Bowl.
Youngblood earned All-Pro honors in
1978 and 1979. (Tennessee Tech.)

FRED ZEIGLER, 1984. The walk-on USC wide receiver from Reevesville (1967–1969) garnered All-ACC honors three times. He led the ACC in receptions in 1967. (University of South Carolina.)

NOT PICTURED

W. N. GRESSETTE, 1990. The St. Matthews native starred at Furman (1913–1918). In 1916, he ran for 318 yards against Erskine College to set a single-game school record that still stands. He also rushed that season for 217 yards against Presbyterian College and 173 against Georgia Tech, with a season total of 865 yards. He held five other records into the 1980s.

2

HOOP HEROES

Basketball can serve as a kind of metaphor for ultimate cooperation. It is a sport where success . . . requires that the dictates of community prevail over selfish personal impulses.

—Bill Bradley

A handful of future South Carolina Athletic Hall of Famers once combined for a remarkable accomplishment: they led the country in scoring for five straight seasons. Furman sharpshooter Frank Selvy and Wofford College seven-footer James E. "Big Daddy" Neal started off the string of national scoring champions in the 1952–1953 season, Selvy in the major-college division, Neal in the NAIA small-college division. With the two schools located about 40 miles apart in Greenville and Spartanburg, the duo wore out the nets in upstate South Carolina. Selvy did it again in 1953–1954. Furman's Darrell Floyd matched his fellow Paladin's feat by topping all NCAA point-producers in 1954–1955 and again in 1955–1956. Then along came Grady Wallace of the University of South Carolina to lead the nation in 1956–1957, capping a remarkable run of individual feats in a team sport.

Still another South Carolina Athletic Hall of Fame inductee turned the trick in 1985 when Columbia native and Wichita State superstar Xavier McDaniel became the first player in NCAA Division I history to lead the nation in both scoring and rebounding. Two years earlier, Columbia native and USC standout Alex English won the NBA scoring title in 1983. English went on to score 2,000 or more points for eight straight NBA seasons, becoming the NBA's leading point-producer of the 1980s. His ability to light up the scoreboard earned his induction into the Basketball Hall of Fame.

Women basketball inductees also share a proclivity for point production. In the 1970s, Pearl Moore, a dynamo scoring machine for Francis Marion College totaled 4,061 points to rank unofficially (women's records were not considered official until later) as college basketball's all-time leader when she ended her career in 1979. Moore has fine company in other female basketball inductees to the South Carolina Athletic Hall of Fame, in the likes of Barbara Kennedy-Dixon of Clemson, Sheila Foster of USC, and Katrina McLain of UGA and Olympic fame.

As for outstanding teams, none gained more spotlight attention than the Frank McGuire era at the University of South Carolina. Those teams include SCAHOF inductees English, John Roche, Tom Owens, Kevin Joyce, Brian Winters, Bobby Cremins, Jim Fox, Gary Gregor, Mike Dunleavy, Jack Thompson, and Skip Harlicka. (Gamecock inductees Wallace and Ronnie Collins starred prior to the arrival of McGuire.)

McDaniel and Tyrone Corbin formed one of the greatest high school tandems in state history while leading Flora High School to the 1981 South Carolina championship before each embarked on a stellar college and NBA career.

Clemson also has enjoyed its share of court standouts in ACC Player of the Year Horace Grant, shot-blocking seven-footer Tree Rollins, NBA Slam Dunk champion Larry Nance, and ABA All Star Randy Mahaffey. Still another ABA All Star, Walt Simon, excelled for tiny Benedict College.

Not all hoop heroes came by their SCAHOF induction via the college or professional route. Legendary Earl Wooten earned his bona fides by dominating the South Carolina Textile League for 20 years.

RALPH BAKER, 1961. From 1912 to 1915, the Prosperity native and three-sport star at Newberry College made All-State twice in football and three times each in basketball and baseball. (Newberry College.)

RONNIE COLLINS, 1999. An all-sports superstar from Winnsboro's Mount Zion High School, Collins went on to become a standout basketball performer at USC (1961–1964) and to lead the Gamecocks in scoring (averaging 23.8 points a game in 1963–1964) and rebounding (8.4 per game in 1961–1962). He made All-ACC in 1964 and All-ACC Tournament in 1962. (University of South Carolina.)

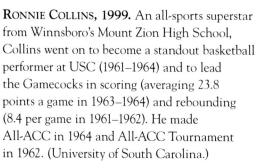

HOOP HEROES

Tyrone Corbin, 2005. The native Columbian first starred at Flora High School, helping the Falcons win the state championship in 1981 before becoming a standout at DePaul University, and then embarking on a long NBA career (1985–2001) as a versatile, all-around performer. The 6-foot-6-inch forward guard averaged 18.0 points a game in 1990–1991 and finished his career with averages of 9.3 points, 4.8 rebounds and 1.8 assists. Since retiring, he has remained in the NBA as an assistant coach. (Minnesota Timberwolves.)

Barbara Kennedy-Dixon, 1998. Clemson's two-time All-American from Rome, Georgia, and three-time All-ACC cager finished her college career as the third-highest all-time NCAA basketball scorer. Dixon went on to play for the 1982 U.S. National team. (Clemson University.)

Mike Dunleavy, 2008. The scrappy 6-foot-2-inch, 175-pound all-purpose guard, a four-year starter, finished his USC career (1972–1976) as the school's number three all-time scorer with 1,586 points. The New Yorker went on to an 11-year NBA career, compiling per-game averages of 8.0 points and 3.9 assists. Dunleavy once scored 48 points off the bench for Milwaukee. Later, as an NBA head coach, Dunleavy led the Los Angeles Lakers to the league finals in 1992, and earned NBA Coach of the Year honors with Portland in 1999 before moving on to the Los Angeles Clippers. (University of South Carolina.)

ALEX ENGLISH, 1993. The only basketball player to start every game of his USC career (111), English scored 1,972 points as a Gamecock (1973–1976) before heading off to a hall of fame career in the NBA. The Columbia native retired with an NBA record of scoring 2,000-or-more points in eight straight seasons. He led the NBA in scoring in 1983 at 28.4 points per game, and scored more points in the 1980s than any other NBA player. (University of South Carolina.)

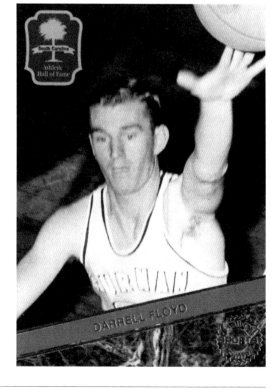

DARRELL FLOYD, 1975. Furman's first two-time first-team basketball All-American and two-time Southern Conference Athlete of Year, Floyd led the nation in scoring in 1955 by averaging 33.8 points a game. He repeated the feat in 1956 with a 35.9 average. The Thomasville, North Carolina, star scored 67 points against Morehouse in 1955. (Furman University.)

HOOP HEROES

SHEILA FOSTER, 2001. USC's two-time All-America post player from Boiling Springs set school records for most career points and rebounds from 1979 to 1982. (University of South Carolina.)

JIM FOX, 2005. This late-bloomer from Sandy Springs, Georgia, came of age as a USC senior during the 1964–1965 season when he led the Gamecocks in scoring (13.6) and rebounding (13.6, second in the ACC) and dominated Clemson with a 30-point and 23-rebounds performance. The 6'10" center went on to enjoy a 10-year NBA career (9.3 points and 7.4 rebounds as per-game career averages) which included a memorable 25-point, 30-rebound game with the Seattle SuperSonics. (University of South Carolina.)

HORACE GRANT, 2009. Clemson's 6-foot-10-inch star won the 1987 ACC Player of the Year when he led the conference in scoring (21.0), rebounding (9.6) and shooting percentage (.656). The second-team All-American from Sparta, Georgia, went on to became a stellar NBA power forward, helping Michael Jordan win three championships (1991–1993) with the Chicago Bulls and in 2001 with the Los Angeles Lakers. He made the 1994 NBA All-Star team and made second-team All-NBA Defensive team four times. The 1987 first-round draft pick shot more than .500 from the field in each of his first 10 NBA seasons, reaching a career-best .578 in 1991–1992. He established career best in 1993–1994 in scoring (15.1), rebounding (11.0) and assists (3.4). (Clemson University.)

GARY GREGOR, 2007. Burly 6-foot-7-inch, 235-pound power forward from Charleston, West Virginia, led ACC in rebounding in 1967–1968 and made All-ACC both years. He played four years in the NBA, making the All-Rookie team in 1968, and two years in the ABA. He averaged 11.1 points and 8.9 rebounds in the pros. (New York Nets.)

Skip Harlicka, 2009. A cornerstone to the success of the McGuire Era at USC along with backcourt mate Jack Thompson, Harlicka led USC in scoring during all three of his varsity seasons (1965–1968), resulting in a 17.5 career average, including 21.8 as a senior, earning him All-ACC and Chuck Taylor Converse All-American honors. The Trenton, New Jersey, native ranks sixth among Gamecocks in per-year career scoring average with 1,209 points. He made the ACC All-Tournament team twice and played a key role in Carolina's rise to the top of the league. He later played for the NBA Atlanta Hawks. (University of South Carolina.)

Kevin Joyce, 1997, and Brian Winters, 1986. Joyce (pictured in the foreground) averaged 17.3 points a game for the Gamecocks over his three-year college career (1971–1973), and helped lead USC to a 69-18 record during that period. In the summer of 1972, Joyce won an Olympic silver medal playing for the United States team at the Munich Olympics. After college, Joyce went on to play in the American Basketball Association. His USC teammate and fellow New Yorker Brian Winters shined in the NBA with the Milwaukee Bucks. A two-time All-Star, Winters averaged 16.2 points a game for his nine-year professional career (1974–1983), and the Bucks retired his jersey after he retired. He later became an NBA head coach. (University of South Carolina.)

RANDY MAHAFFEY, 2003. Named first-team All-ACC for Clemson in 1967, Mahaffey went on to become an ABA All-Star in 1968. The LaGrange, Georgia, native averaged 12 points a game for his 321-game professional career, which spanned from 1967 to 1971. (Clemson University.)

XAVIER MCDANIEL, 2003. The Columbia native led Flora High School to the South Carolina state basketball title in 1981. "X-Man" later became a first-team All-American at Wichita State where he led the nation in scoring (27) and rebounding (14.8) in 1985. He went on to become an NBA All-Star. (Seattle SuperSonics.)

KATRINA MCLAIN, 2006. Charleston native and three-time basketball All-American at the University of Georgia (where she set several records, and won National Player of the Year honors in 1987); McLain starred for U.S. Olympic teams in 1988, 1992, and 1996 and was inducted into the Women's Basketball Hall of Fame in 2006. (University of Georgia.)

Pearl Moore, 2000. A basketball phenom in the 1970s when women's records were not yet formally kept, the 5-foot-5-inch Francis Marion star from Florence is unofficially ranked as the most prolific scorer in college basketball history, male or female, having racked up a total of 4,061 points by the time she ended her college career in 1979. The four-time All-American once scored 60 points in an AIAW tournament game. After college, Moore extended her career by playing several years of professional ball in the United States and South America. (Francis Marion University.)

James E. "Big Daddy" Neal, 1990. The Wofford basketball seven-footer from Silverstreet dominated his era. As a senior in 1952–1953, he averaged 32.6 points a game, and led the NAIA in rebounding (28 per game) before playing briefly in the NBA. (Wofford College.)

Larry Nance, 2001. The Clemson star from Anderson won the NBA's first Slam Dunk Contest in 1984 and made the All-Star team a year later. In 1994, he retired as the NBA's all-time shot-blocking and percentage-shooting forward. (Clemson University.)

TOM OWENS, 1991, AND BOBBY CREMINS, 1988. Tom Owens (No. 24 in the background), a USC basketball star from 1969 to 1971, is the only Gamecock player to compile 1,000 points and 1,000 rebounds in three different seasons. The All-ACC star averaged 15.8 points and led the league in rebounding three times, averaging a career 13.3 boards; he spent 12 years in the pros with nine teams in the ABA and NBA, averaging 11.3 points and 6.1 rebounds. Fellow New Yorker Bobby Cremins (No. 21) was a scrappy and beloved USC basketball player (1968–1970) who captained the Gamecocks in 1970 and went on to coach at Appalachian State, Georgia Tech, and College of Charleston. He made the Yellow Jackets an ACC and national basketball power. (University of South Carolina.)

FRANK SELVY, 1960. This two-time Southern Conference Player of the Year and 1954 consensus All-American from Corbin, Kentucky, twice led the nation in scoring at Furman (1952–1953 and 1953–1954) and set a NCAA single-game record of 100 points. He is a charter member of the South Carolina Athletic Hall of Fame and the Southern Conference Hall of Fame. (Furman University.)

HOOP HEROES

JOHN ROCHE, 1983. Widely considered the greatest basketball player in USC history, Roche averaged 22.5 points and led the team to a 69-16 record from 1969 to 1971, while winning ACC Player of Year and All-American honors. The New York native later played in the ABA and NBA from 1972 to 1981. (University of South Carolina.)

WAYNE "TREE" ROLLINS, 2002. The three-time All-ACC performer from Cordele, Georgia, and 1977 All-American at Clemson (1973–1977) became a premier shot-blocking center in 18 years in the NBA. (Clemson University.)

WALT SIMON, 1997. Benedict College's basketball star from Delcambre, Louisiana, was picked No. 1 in the initial ABA draft in 1967. In his second season, the spindly forward averaged 21.1 and scored 18 points in the All-Star Game. (Simon family.)

JACK THOMPSON, 2009. The slick ball-handling guard from Brooklyn, New York, widely regarded as the best passer in USC history, Thompson averaged 10.9 points but scored when he had to, as he did in making 10 of 12 shots at Duke to hold the highest shooting percentage by a Duke opponent for 24 years. He became a building block for the hugely successful McGuire Era. Thompson made second-team All-ACC as well as All-ACC tournament twice and All-South Carolina twice. He played briefly for the ABA Indiana Pacers. The University of South Carolina named its Playmaker of the Year Award in Thompson's name. (University of South Carolina.)

GRADY WALLACE, 1976. A consensus All-American at USC when he led nation in scoring in 1957 with a school-record 31.3 average, Wallace also holds the school record for career average (28.0). In 1955, the Mare Creek, Kentucky, native led all junior college scorers at 32.8. (University of South Carolina.)

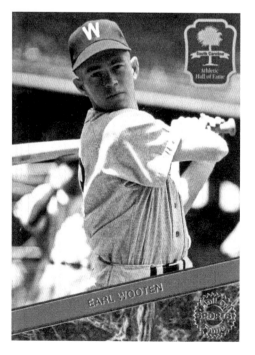

EARL WOOTEN, 1962. After a brief major league baseball career, "The Pride of Pelzer" became a Southern Textile Basketball League legend 1941–1961, making all-tournament 12 times. Although unofficial, he holds career records for most points and highest average. (Wooten family.)

3

DIAMOND DANDIES

You got to be a man to play baseball for a living,
but you got to have a lot of little boy in you, too.

—Roy Campanella

A baseball manager with a roster of South Carolina Athletic Hall of Famers might put together a formidable "fantasy" lineup since all starred at various levels, many in Major League Baseball.

One could not go wrong by naming Bobby Richardson in the leadoff spot and naming him as team captain. The former New York Yankees' All-Star second baseman and World Series hero would, no doubt, set the tone and spirit of our mythical squad.

Toss in Mookie Wilson and Wayne Tolleson for base-stealing speed, and pick from among plenty of pure hitters such as Shoeless Joe Jackson, Larry Doby, and Rusty Adkins, and then add thunder in the likes of sluggers Jim Rice of the Baseball Hall of Fame, Gorman Thomas, and Al Rosen. For versatility, blend in Bill Spiers, Ty Cline, and Jerry Martin. For defense, rely on Marty Marion, Chick Galloway, and Don Buddin.

The pitching staff, caught by Sydney Smith, would not lack arms. Choose from among old-time workhorses from the 1930s and 1940s such as Bobo Newsome (one of baseball's all-time colorful characters), Kirby Higbe, Van Lingle Mungo and Lou Brissie; or aces from the 1950s such as Tom Brewer and Billy O'Dell, or fireballers from the 1960s (Bob Bolin), or control artists from the 1980s (LaMarr Hoyt, Earl Bass) or an All-Star from the 1990s (Jimmy Key).

RUSTY ADKINS, 1995. The Clemson baseball great (1964–1967) from Fort Mill batted .444 in 1965 and had a career .379 average. He made All-State, All-ACC and All-American for three years and set conference records for most at-bats without a strikeout and longest hitting streak (41 games). He is a member of the Clemson's Ring of Honor. (Clemson University.)

EARL BASS, 2000. A native of Columbia, the two-time USC All-ACC and All-American (1974–1975) pitched his way to a 34-3 record in a little over two seasons of college ball. Bass holds host of school marks, including most consecutive victories (23, at one time a national record). In 1975, he logged a 17-1 record and finished runner-up for the Lefty Gomez Plate, given to amateur baseball's top player. (University of South Carolina.)

BOB BOLIN, 2008. The fireballer from Hickory Grove pitched in the Major Leagues for 13 years with an 88-75 record, with 50 saves and a 3.40 ERA. In 1968, he ranked second in the NL with 1.99 ERA. In 1964, Bolin ranked sixth in strikeouts per nine innings at 7.52. In 1965, he went 14-6 (fourth in winning percentage), ranked seventh in ERA (2.76), and struck out 135 batters in 163 innings. (San Francisco Giants.)

TOM BREWER, 1985. The three-sport star at Cheraw High School and major league All-Star pitcher for the Boston Red Sox recorded a 91-82 eight-year career record, including 19-9 mark in 1956 when he made the AL All-Star team. For his career, he pitched 13 shutouts and 75 complete games in 217 starts. Before retiring with an arm injury, he ranked tenth all-time in Boston victories and strikeouts. (Boston Red Sox.)

LOU BRISSIE, 1974. The Anderson native went from playing at Presbyterian College as a basketball and baseball standout (1941–1943) to fighting in World War II. He returned with extensive leg injuries. Nevertheless, he defied the odds and became a major league pitcher, making the All-Rookie team in 1948 and the American League All-Star team in 1949. Pitching for the Philadelphia Athletics and the Cleveland Indians, he compiled a lifetime 44-48 career record with a 4.07 ERA and 436 strikeouts. Brissie later became a MLB scout with the Dodgers and Braves, and then director of the American Legion baseball program. His biography, *The Corporal Was a Pitcher*, came out in 2009. (Brissie family.)

DON BUDDIN, 1996. The All-American high school star from Olanta High School started varsity baseball in the sixth grade and never lost a game in six seasons as a pitcher. He became a major league shortstop (1956–1963) and—playing for the Boston Red Sox—four times led the American League in putouts, assists, and double plays; he finished his career with a .241 lifetime batting average. (Buddin family.)

TY CLINE, 2009. He starred at Clemson (1956–1960) as an outfielder and pitcher. In 1960, the Hampton native made All-ACC, All-Atlantic Region and All-American. In 1959, he helped the Tigers advance to College World Series, and he played for the U.S. Pan Am team. He hit .335 for his college career, then went on to play 12 years in the majors. He spearheaded two key victories for Cincinnati over Pittsburgh in the 1970 National League Championship Series. He is a member of the Charleston Hall of Fame. (Clemson University.)

LARRY DOBY, 1973. Born in Camden, Doby became a member of the Baseball Hall of Fame in 1998. The first black player ever to play in the American League, Doby led the AL in home runs in 1952 and 1954 (32 each year), and led the league in RBI in 1954 (126). He hit 253 home runs and batted .283 over his 13-year career, playing with Cleveland, the Chicago White Sox, and Detroit. In two World Series, he hit .318. In six All-Star Games, Doby hit one home run and batted .300 (Cleveland Indians.)

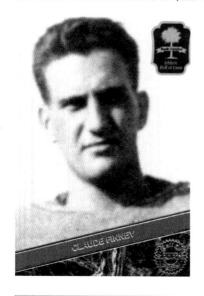

CLAUDE FINNEY, 1961. The Wofford football and baseball star made All-SIAA in 1928. (Wofford College.)

ART FOWLER, 1996. The Converse-born pitcher (1954–1964) compiled a career 54-51 record for the Reds, Dodgers, and Angels, but is probably best known as much-traveled manager Billy Martin's pitching coach for five different ball clubs, including three different stints with the New York Yankees. One of Fowler's most famous protégés was Ron Guidry, who won the Cy Young Award in 1978. (New York Yankees.)

CHICK GALLOWAY, 1976. This Manning native became a star athlete and coach at Presbyterian College and enjoyed fine major league career (1921–1926), hitting for a career high .324 in 1922 and compiling a .264 career average as starting shortstop with the Philadelphia A's. He later suited up for Detroit. His career ended prematurely when he suffered a fractured skull in batting practice. He later scouted for the Reds, A's, and Braves. (Presbyterian College.)

VIOLA THOMPSON-GRIFFIN, 1997. The Carolina Upstate native starred in the All-American Girls Professional Baseball League (made famous in the 1992 film, *A League of Their Own,*) from 1944 to 1947. "Tommie" played for the World Series championship team Milwaukee Chicks in 1944. She went on to play in the National Girls Baseball League from 1948 to 1951. (Thompson-Griffin family.)

KIRBY HIGBE, 1984. The Columbia native compiled a 118-101 record as a major league pitcher from 1937–1950. The two-time All-Star (1940 and 1946) led the NL in strikeouts in 1940 and in victories in 1941 with a 22-9 record. He recorded a .648 winning percentage against first-division teams while with the Dodgers. After retiring, he returned to Columbia to coach the Post Six American Legion team from 1957–1960. (Higbe family.)

LaMARR HOYT, 2006. The Columbia native became a fire-balling MLB pitcher with career 98-69 record with 3.66 ERA. In 1983, he went 24-10 for White Sox and won the American League Cy Young Award. In 1985 with San Diego, he started the All-Star Game and won the game's MVP Award. (Chicago White Sox.)

"SHOELESS" JOE JACKSON, 1969. Born in Greenville, Jackson started as a mill team player and starred for 13 years in the major leagues. He hit for a .356 career average and played in the World Series in 1917 and 1919 with the Chicago White Sox. Most baseball historians consider him to be among the game's all-time greatest hitters. He received his famous nickname after playing the second game of a minor league doubleheader in Anderson in his stockings because a new pair of spikes had given him blisters in the first game. In 1921, a Chicago jury acquitted him of aiding a fix to the 1919 World Series, but the baseball commissioner went against the court's decision and banned Joe and seven other White Sox players for life. The ban has kept him out of the National Baseball Hall of Fame at Cooperstown, N.Y. Veteran former players and fans alike have called the ban an injustice and campaigned to end it. Joe's legendary 48-ounce, 36-inch "Black Betsy" bat sold in 2001 for $577,610 at auction. (Chicago White Sox.)

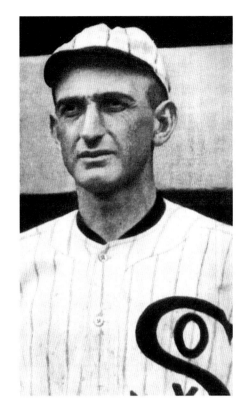

JIMMY KEY, 2006. An All-ACC pitcher from Huntsville, Alabama, and designated hitter in 1982 for Clemson, Key moved on to a storied major league career from 1984 to 1998, with a 186-117 record, and a lifetime 3.15 ERA. He earned All-Star Game honors four times, and helped Toronto win the World Series in 1992. (New York Yankees.)

ELIZABETH "LIB" MAHON, 2005. The Greenville native and two-time all star (1946 and 1949) in the All-American Girls Professional Baseball League twice led the league in RBIs, and ranks fourth all-time in AAGPBL career RBIs with 400. (Mahon family.)

MARTY MARION, 1969. The Richborg native became a defensive whiz at shortstop for the St. Louis Cardinals and Browns from 1940 to 1955; he led the National League in fielding three times, made seven All-Star teams and won the 1944 National League MVP award. (St. Louis Cardinals.)

JAMES "PEPPER" MARTIN, 1981. The Furman football, basketball and baseball star (1938–1941) made All-State in three sports and All-Southern Conference in baseball, and later played five years in minor league baseball. (Furman University.)

JERRY MARTIN, 2007. The four-sport star at Columbia's Olympia High School shined in baseball and basketball at Spartanburg Junior College and Furman University (1970–1971) and went on to enjoy an 11-year major league playing career with the Phillies and Cubs, and a long coaching career in professional ball. (Philadelphia Phillies.)

VAN LINGLE MUNGO, 1974. The Pageland native who never lost a high school game pitched for 14 years in the major leagues (1931–1945) and compiled a career 120-115 record with 16 saves. In his first game, he struck out 12 batters, and he led the National League in strikeouts with 238 in 1937. His name is used as the title of a song by Dave Frishberg. (Mungo family.)

BILLY O'DELL, 1976. A left-handed pitcher from Whitmire who played for Clemson University, O'Dell made All-Southern Conference in 1952 and 1953 and All-American in 1954, and pitched a no-hitter against USC. He also played three years of football for Clemson before moving on to an outstanding major league baseball career. The MVP of the 1958 All-Star Game played in the 1962 World Series for the Giants and compiled a lifetime 105-100, 3.29 ERA from 1954 to 1967. (Clemson University.)

JIM RICE, 1990. This Anderson native became an All-Star with the Boston Red Sox, winning the American League MVP award in 1978. He batted .298 for his career, hit 382 home runs, and led the American League in homers three times. He earned induction into the National Baseball Hall of Fame in 2009. (Boston Red Sox.)

BOBBY RICHARDSON, 1968. The Sumter-born, slick-fielding second baseman for the New York Yankees during the Mantle and Maris era, Richardson played in seven World Series and seven All Star Games from 1955-1966, batting for a career .266 average. In 1960, he was the World Series MVP and set the series record with 12 runs batted in. In seven World Series with the Yankees, Richardson hit for a .305 lifetime average. Richardson later coached USC (1970–1976) to a 220-91-2 record, took the Gamecocks to three NCAA playoffs, and finished second in nation in 1975 with 51-6-1 mark. (New York Yankees.)

AL ROSEN, 1978. The Spartanburg native hit .285 over a long major league career (1947–1956), was named an All-Star four times, and won the 1953 American League Most Valuable Player award when he hit 43 home runs and drove in 145. He later became a front-office executive with the New York Yankees, Houston Astros, and San Francisco Giants. (Cleveland Indians.)

BILL SPIERS, 2007. Cameron native Bill Spiers journeyed to Clemson (1985–1987) to become first-team All-American and an All-ACC baseball star. He punted for Tigers' football team before embarking on a 13-year major league baseball career, which he concluded with a .271 average. Primarily an infielder, Spiers made versatility a prime ingredient of his resume. (Clemson University.)

GORMAN THOMAS, 2004. The power-hitting centerfielder played most of his career with the Milwaukee Brewers, and led the American League in home runs in 1979 and 1982. Over his 13-year career, Thomas hit 268 home runs and drove in 782 runs. The Johns Island native hit more homers between 1979 and 1982 than anyone else in baseball, and played in the 1981 All-Star Game. (Milwaukee Brewers.)

WAYNE TOLLESON, 2010. Tolleson starred in football and baseball at Spartanburg High School and Western Carolina University, and played 10 seasons of Major League Baseball (1981–1990). At WCU, he led the nation in 1978 in pass receiving and, the same school year, earned Southern Conference honors as the league's baseball player and overall athlete of the year. As a major league infielder, Tolleson batted .241 for his career and had a .972 fielding percentage while playing for the Rangers, White Sox, and Yankees. He enjoyed his best season in 1985 (.313, 21 stolen bases). (Western Carolina University.)

FRITZ VON KOLNITZ, 1961. The Charleston native played football and baseball at USC (1911–1913) and in 115 major league games from 1914 to 1916 with the Cincinnati Reds and Chicago White Sox. (Safran Antiques.)

ERNIE WHITE, 1978. The Pacolet native played (with fellow SCAHOF-member Marty Marion) for the St. Louis Cardinals from 1940–1943, going 17-7 in 1941 and pitching a crucial complete-game shutout against the Yankees in the third game of the 1942 World Series. After the Cardinals completed their series victory, White took three years off to fight in World War II (including the Battle of the Bulge), and returned to pitch for the Boston Braves from 1946-1948. In a seven-year career, White recorded an overall 30-21 pitching record and 2.78 ERA. He went on to serve as General Manager of the Columbia Reds minor league team. (South Carolina Athletic Hall of Fame.)

MOOKIE WILSON, 1995. The speedy, Bamberg-born switch hitter starred at Bamberg High and Spartanburg Methodist Junior College, then led USC to the 1977 College World Series before moving on to a major league career, culminating in a 1986 World Series title with the New York Mets. (The famous "Buckner Ball"—the grounder that famously rolled under Red Sox Bill Buckner's glove in Game 6—was hit by Wilson). Over his 12-year career, Wilson compiled a .274 average with 327 stolen bases. (New York Mets.)

LEWIS NORMAN "BOBO" NEWSOM, 1969. Newsom came out of Hartsville to pitch 20 years in the major leagues for nine different teams, appearing in more than 600 games with a lifetime 211-222 record, oftentimes laboring for poor clubs. The 6-foot-2-inch, 220-pound colorful character referred to everyone—including himself—as "Bobo" (example: "Bobo pitched a good game today.") He led the American League in strikeouts in 1942, and four times led the league in Games Started, and twice in Complete Games. He was a four-time All Star, and could win consistently when he had the support: he won 20 or more games three times. (Detroit Tigers.)

NOT PICTURED

SYDNEY SMITH, 1962. The Smithfield-born USC football and baseball standout played in the major leagues as a catcher from 1908 to 1915. The Camden native also ranked as a six-goal polo layer, and coached the Citadel's first football team in 1905.

4

GALAXY OF GREATS

The most important thing is to love your sport.
Never do it to please someone else. It has to be yours.

—Peggy Fleming

Beyond the so-called major sports of football, basketball and baseball, South Carolina has been blessed with an array of outstanding sports figures, many with national or even international name recognition.

Luminaries such as Wimbledon tennis champion and racial pioneer Althea Gibson, heavyweight boxing champion "Smokin' Joe" Frazier; NASCAR champion drivers David Pearson and Cale Yarborough; LPGA stars Betsy Rawls, Beth Daniel, and Betsy King; tennis standout Stan Smith, and legendary Thoroughbred racehorse trainers Max Hirsch and Frank Whiteley all rank among the giants in their fields, all chosen for induction into their sports' respective national halls of fame.

Three South Carolina Athletic Hall of Fame inductees rose to international heights in their chosen endeavors. Dr. Leroy Walker, the former Benedict track star, coached the 1976 Olympic track team and later served as a longtime Olympic administrator. P. J. Boatwright, likewise, became known as the world's foremost authority on the Rules of Golf. Lucille "Ludy" Godbold won two gold medals in the 1922 Olympics. Bud Moore, a World War II hero from Spartanburg, invented many safety measures for his sport of auto racing.

BUCK BAKER, 2003. The NASCAR star of the 1950s won three Southern 500s (1953, 1960, 1964) among his 46 Grand National victories, and two Grand National point championships (1956, 1957). The Richborg native also won hundreds of short-track races. He is a member of the North Carolina Sports Hall of Fame and two motor sports shrines. (NASCAR.)

BUDDY BAKER, 1988. Elzie Wylie "Buddy" Baker, also nicknamed "Leadfoot" for his pedal-to-metal style, starred as a NASCAR driver from 1967 to 1992. The Florence native (and son of Buck Baker), became the first driver to run 200-plus miles per hour in a stock car on an enclosed course when he drove 200.447 at Talladega in 1970. He won the 1980 Daytona 500 and had 19 career victories and 311 top ten finishes. He is a member of the International Motorsports and the National Motorsports Press Association Halls of Fame as well as the Charlotte Motor Speedway Court of Legends. (NASCAR.)

GALAXY OF GREATS

GRANT BENNETT, 1980. The legendary youth golf teacher coached Florence McClenaghan High School to six state championships and seven Southern titles from 1951 to 1964. He conceived and built the Country Club of South Carolina at Florence. The dedicated SCAHOF past president (1993) worked long and hard to find a home for the organization. He also is a member of the South Carolina Golf, Carolinas Golf, and Carolinas PGA Halls of Fame. (Bennett family.)

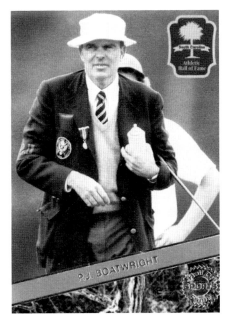

P. J. BOATWRIGHT JR., 1976. A product of Spartanburg, this two-time Carolina Open champion (1957, 1959) and Wofford College star qualified for four U.S. amateurs. Later a respected national golf administrator as Executive Director of the USGA (1969–1991), Boatwright became known as the world's foremost authority on the Rules of Golf. He is member of the South Carolina Golf and Carolinas Halls of Fame. (USGA.)

JACK CHANDLER, 1985. The Clemson track and basketball standout from 1923-25 never lost a 100-yard dash throughout his college career. (Clemson University.)

JANE COVINGTON, 1973. The Orangeburg native, five-time CGA champion, and five-time South Carolina champ dominated women's amateur golf in the Carolinas from late 1940s to mid-1960s. She is a member of the South Carolina Golf Hall of Fame. (Covington family.)

CAROLYN CUDONE, 1975. The women's golf star won 48 major titles (1950–1974), including five USGA National Senior crowns, five Carolinas Golf Association Medal Play championships, and four South Carolina Golf Association Medal Play titles. She captained the U.S. Curtis Cup team and is in the South Carolina Golf Hall of Fame. (Cudone family.)

BETH DANIEL, 1978. Twice won U.S. Women's Amateur (1975, 1977) and led Furman to NCAA championship to become SCAHOF's youngest inductee at age 20; went on to become three-time LPGA Player of Year and three-time leading money winners (1980, 1981, 1990). The Charleston native won the 1976 LPGA tournament and finished second in five other majors, and record 25 top ten finished in majors. She is a member of the LPGA, World Golf, and South Carolina Golf Halls of Fame. (Furman University.)

SAM DANIEL, 1973. USC's tennis courts are named after this 1930s perennial South Carolina Open singles champ. He is also a member of the South Carolina Tennis Hall of Fame. (University of South Carolina.)

MAC FOLGER, 1993. Clemson's football and track star (1933–1936) set the South Carolina record in the 220-yard low hurdles with a time of 23.5. (Clemson University.)

FRANK FORD, 1995. A standout golfer from Charleston who won seven South Carolina Amateur titles from 1930 to 1950, Ford also finished runner-up three times, and won the 1937 International 4-Ball title. He is a member of the Carolinas Golf and South Carolina Golf Halls of Fame. (Ford family.)

"Smokin' Joe" Frazier, 1974. The Beaufort native won an Olympic gold medal in 1964 and became the world heavyweight boxing champion in 1968. He lives forever in boxing annals for his classic ring battles against Muhammad Ali in 1971, 1974, and 1975. He compiled a 32-4-1 professional record and is enshrined in the Pro Boxing Hall of Fame. (Safran Antiques.)

Althea Gibson, 1983. The native of Silver opened doors for black athletes in tennis and in golf. She won 10 consecutive ATA national championships, and went on to conquer both Wimbledon and the U.S. Open in 1957 and 1958, and won three Wimbledon Doubles championships among her 11 major titles and 56 crowns overall. She earned the AP Women's Athlete of Year (1957 and 1958) and Babe Zaharias Award for the most outstanding female athlete. The Florida A&M Athlete of the Century, Gibson was named to the *Sports Illustrated* Top 100 Greatest Female Athletes list and is a member of several halls of fame (International Tennis, National Lawn, International Women, New Jersey, Florida, and Black Athletes). She titled her 1958 autobiography, *I Always Wanted to Be Somebody*. (Gibson family.)

GALAXY OF GREATS

RANDY GLOVER, 1982. This Cheraw native won eight South Carolina Opens, seven Carolinas PGA Player of Year awards, and played on three PGA Cup Match Play teams. He is a member of the South Carolina Golf Hall of Fame. (Glover family.)

LUCILLE GODBOLD, 1961. The first female SCAHOF inductee set three track records at Winthrop College in the 1920s. She set the women's world shot put record at the Paris International track meet in 1922, won the gold in the triple jump, and collected four other medals as well. Columbia College, her longtime teaching and coaching venue and the site of the annual Ludy Bowl, which she herself started in 1950, named its gymnasium after the beloved "Miss Ludy." (Columbia College.)

JAY HAAS, 2005. The Greer native starred at Wake Forest and went on to win nine PGA tournaments and three Ryder Cups. He finished third in the 1995 Masters Tournament, and second in the 2003 PGA before becoming a force on the senior tour. He was a 2007 inductee to the South Carolina Golf Hall of Fame. (Professional Golf Association.)

PAUL HAHN, 1976. This trick-shot golf artist from Charleston has entertained fans around the world. Known as golf's ambassador at large, Hahn entertained fans at Augusta National and St. Andrews as well as American troops abroad. (South Carolina Athletic Hall of Fame.)

KATHRYN HEMPHILL, 1974. This native Columbian was a three-time SCGA champion; she won the Texas Open in 1939, the Mexican National Championship in 1936–1937, and played for the Curtis Cup team in 1938. She is a member of the South Carolina Golf Hall of Fame (Hemphill family.)

JANIE HAYNIE HENTZ, 1987. The Belton native became a five-time girls' high school tennis singles champion in the 1950s. The Converse College standout ranked number one in the South and eighth in the nation in 1956 in the age 18 division; she won women's opens in South Carolina, North Carolina, and Georgia in 1955–1956, and twice won the Lewis Teague Award as the best female athlete in the Carolinas. Later she was the first female inducted into the South Carolina Tennis Hall of Fame. (Hentz family.)

MAX HIRSCH, 1997. A legendary racehorse trainer from Fredericksburg, Texas, and based out of Columbia beginning in the 1930s, Hirsch won the Triple Crown in 1946 with Assault. His horses won the Kentucky Derby three times, the Preakness twice, and the Belmont four times, He is enshrined in the National Thoroughbred Racing Hall of Fame. (Hirsch family.)

COURTNEY SHEALY HART, 2010. The Irmo native won two U.S. Olympic gold medals in swimming (400-meter relay and 400-freestyle relay) in 2000. She led the University of Georgia to the NCAA team swim championships in 1999 and 2000. In 2000, she earned NCAA female Swimmer of the Year honors after winning national titles in the 50-meter freestyle, 100-meter freestyle and 100-meter backstroke. She also won NCAA titles in the 400-meter freestyle and 400-meter medley relay teams. Hart also excelled in volleyball at Irmo High and at the University of Georgia. (United States Olympic Committee.)

KATHY HITE, 1991. The Florence sub junior golf champion in 1961–1962, Hite won the South Carolina Interscholastic title and South Carolina Women's crown in 1969, and finished seventh in the U.S. Amateur before playing on the LPGA tour. She is a member of the South Carolina Golf Hall of Fame. (Hite family.)

BETSY KING, 1992. King led Furman to the NCAA Women's National Championship in 1976. A three-time LPGA Player of the Year (1984, 1989, 1993), King led the tour in earnings three times and won six majors—including the U.S. Open in 1989 and 1990 and the British Open in 1992. She was inducted into World Golf Hall of Fame in 1995. (Furman University.)

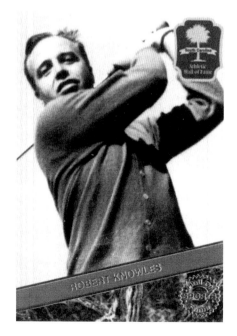

BOBBY KNOWLES, 1985. The Massachusetts native and longtime Aiken resident twice won South Carolina Amateur, South Carolina Senior Amateur, and Carolinas Senior tournaments. The 1950 U.S. Amateur semifinalist won the French Amateur in 1951 and played on the 1951 Walker Cup team. He is a South Carolina Golf Hall of Fame member. (Knowles family.)

GALAXY OF GREATS

TINA KREBS, 2003. The distance star track competitor at Clemson (1983 and 1985–1987) and six-time Tigers' All-American won three NCAA indoor titles: the 1,000 meter; the 1,500 meter; and the mile. The Holbaek, Denmark, native is a member of the Clemson Ring of Honor. (Clemson University.)

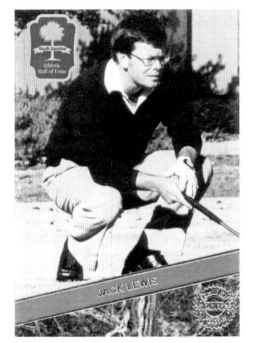

JACK LEWIS, 1987. Florence native led McClenaghan High School to five Southern Intercollegiate and four state championships and won the Carolinas Golf Association crown three times. He became a two-time All-American at Wake Forest (1968 and 1969), won the ACC golf title in 1968, and played three years on the PGA tour (1970–1973). He is a South Carolina Golf Hall of Famer. (Lewis family.)

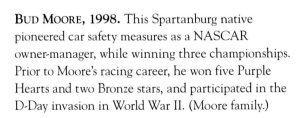

BUD MOORE, 1998. This Spartanburg native pioneered car safety measures as a NASCAR owner-manager, while winning three championships. Prior to Moore's racing career, he won five Purple Hearts and two Bronze stars, and participated in the D-Day invasion in World War II. (Moore family.)

ALLEN MORRIS, 2004. A Presbyterian College tennis star and three-time Davis Cup alternate (1944, 1955, 1956) reached the Wimbledon quarterfinals in 1956, and that year was ranked number 14 in the world. The Atlanta native and former University of North Carolina tennis coach is a member of six halls of fame. (Presbyterian College.)

F. W. "GUNNER" OHLANDT, 1990. Ohlandt captained the Citadel's football and boxing teams. He won the Southern Conference heavyweight title in 1947 and held it until 1949, and won the league light-heavyweight crown in 1950, finishing with a 114-3 college record. (Citadel.)

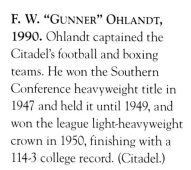

GALAXY OF GREATS

EVERETT "COTTON" OWENS, 2009. The native of Union gained fame as the "King of the Modifieds" as a driver. As a crew chief, he won a Grand National championship with David Pearson and teamed with Buddy Baker to win the 1970 Southern 500. The Stock Car Racing Hall of Fame at Darlington inducted Owens in 1970. In 1998, he was named one of NASCAR's 50 Greatest Drivers. He has been honored with Lifetime Achievement in Auto Racing and Pioneer Racing awards, and has been inducted into the International Motorsports Hall of Fame. (NASCAR.)

DAVID PEARSON, 1973. The Spartanburg native, nicknamed "The Silver Fox" for his sly track maneuvers, won the NASCAR championship in 1966, 1968, and 1969. He was elected to the International Motorsports Hall of Fame in 1990, and to the Motorsports Hall of Fame in 1993. (NASCAR.)

DOTTIE PEPPER, 2008. A three-time golf All-American at Furman before winning 17 LPGA tournaments, including two majors, Pepper from Saratoga Springs, New York, led the LPGA in victories in 1992 and 1996, and played on five Solheim Cup teams. (Ladies Professional Golf Association.)

HENRY PICARD, 1977. A club golf professional in Charleston (1925–1934), Picard won 26 PGA Tour events including the 1938 Masters. In 1939, the Plymouth, Massachusetts, native won the 1939 PGA Championship and led the PGA in earnings. "Pick" is a member of the South Carolina and World Golf Halls of Fame. (Picard family.)

ALLEN POWERS, 2000. The All-American golfer at USC (1966–1968) was known for his prodigious tee shots. Powers set six club records and won six Carolinas Golf Association championships. He is a member of the South Carolina Golf Hall of Fame. (South Carolina Golf Association.)

BETSY RAWLS, 1962. The Spartanburg native won 55 LPGA tournaments, including eight majors and four Women's National Opens from 1951 to 1975. She is one of the LPGA's founders, its first president (1961–1967), and a charter inductee into the LPGA Tour Hall of Fame in 1967. She is a South Carolina Golf Hall of Famer and was the second female SCAHOF inductee. (Ladies Professional Golf Association.)

LILLIAN PAILLE SEABROOK, 1979. The standout Charleston tennis player from 1924 to 1977 won 173 tournaments and earned induction into the South Carolina Tennis Hall of Fame in 1985. (Seabrook family.)

JOHN SIMPSON, 1983. The Chester native won more than 1,500 races and $5 million in purses in harness racing as a trainer-driver (1936–1972). He won the Hambletonian twice and the Little Brown Jug three times, and is a member of the Trotters Hall of Fame. (Simpson family.)

         GALAXY OF GREATS

STAN SMITH, 2010. The California native has been a Hilton Head resident since the 1970s; he won the U.S. Open singles in 1971 and Wimbledon singles in 1972, and ranks among all-time tennis greats. He teamed to win 54 doubles championships, including five grand slams (U.S. Open in 1968, 1974, 1978, 1980 and the Australian Open in 1970). The three-time All-American won the 1968 NCAA singles championship, and doubles titles in 1967–1968, and made 10 Davis Cup appearances. He has been inducted into the South Carolina Tennis Hall of Fame (1985) and the International Tennis HOF (1987). (Smith family.)

DR. LEROY WALKER, 1977. A Little All-American at Benedict College where he starred in football, basketball, and track, Walker became a 1976 U.S. Olympic track coach and has served as a longtime Olympic administrator and organizer. The Atlanta native is a member of 16 halls of fame, including the National Track and Field Hall of Fame and the U.S. Olympic Hall of Fame. (USA Track and Field.)

FRANK WHITELEY, 1998. The legendary Camden Thoroughbred trainer (1936–1984) trained all-time great filly Ruffian as well as champions Forego and Damascus, among his 35 stakes winners. The Centreville, Maryland, native is a member of National Thoroughbred Racing Hall of Fame. (Camden Archives.)

CALE YARBOROUGH, 1978. The Timmonsville native became NASCAR's only three-in-a-row champion driver (1976–1978). He won 83 races (fifth all-time), including the Daytona 500 four times. In 1993, Yarborough was inducted into the International Motorsports Hall of Fame in 1993 and a year later was named to the Motorsports Hall of Fame. (NASCAR.)

5

COACHING CHAMPIONS

Coaches who can outline plays on a blackboard are a dime a dozen.
The ones who win get inside their players and motivate.

—Vince Lombardi

Where to start?

When reviewing the roll of coaches in the South Carolina Athletic Hall of Fame, do you start with John McKissick, the state's (and, in fact, the *world*'s) all-time winningest football coach? Or Frank Howard—arguably, its most colorful? Or Danny Ford, the only one to win a major college football national championship? Or Frank McGuire, who brought the most sustained and exciting era of athletic success that the University of South Carolina has ever known? Or John Kresse, who established remarkable longtime basketball excellence at the small college level (and won a national championship in the process)? Or Dick Sheridan, whose teams often dominated those of his peers despite the fact that he was given less talent to work with? Or Fisher DeBerry, who took military academy football to remarkable success? Or how about John Heisman, so famous for excellence that college football named its most coveted trophy for him.

What about the state's group of unbelievably successful women's coaches? Or a racial pioneer like Willie Jeffries? Or soccer pioneer I. M. Ibrahim? Or such track legends as Weems Baskin or Howard Bagwell? Or a contingent of father-like high school coaches who won big-time while sharing important life lessons with their players? Or ones who succeeded in the professional ranks? Or those who simply won often, and did it with exceptional class?

All of the above would do. But collectively, they form a preponderance of superlative mentors. So let's start with the most humble. Stan Zuk, an All-American fullback at Columbia University who carried his Ivy League education to namesake Columbia, South Carolina, where he took the perhaps the most low profile and rewarding of positions—serving as father figure/coach of the Epworth Orphanage football team, compiling a 53-5-3 record.

GENE ALEXANDER, 1975. The NAIA Hall of Famer coached basketball at Wofford and Erskine and ranks as one of the NAIA's winningest coaches, with more than 450 career victories. (Wofford College.)

LYLES ALLEY, 1968. After playing football, basketball, and baseball for Furman, Lyles Alley went on to coach the Paladins' basketball team from 1945 to 1966, winning 223 games; his innovative offensive system produced national scoring champions for four straight years in the 1950s. (Furman University.)

PINKY BABB, 1973. The legendary Greenwood High School football coach began in 1942 and coached for 40 years, ending with a lifetime 346-85-25 record. Babb was the first high school coach inducted to the SCAHOF. A former All-State football player at Furman, Babb coached nine state championship teams. He is also a member of the Furman College and the National High School Coaches Association Halls of Fame. The Greenwood High School football field is named in his honor. (Babb family.)

HOWARD BAGWELL, 1966. A renowned track coach at Charleston Southern University (1965–2000) with a 263-47 record and four state track championships, the Big South Hall of Famer started the school's athletic programs in the days when it was called Baptist College. (Charleston Southern University.)

ART BAKER, 1995. A Sumter native who excelled as a high school football coach at Eau Claire High School in 1959 and 1960, Baker moved on to college ranks as head coach at Furman (1973–1977), the Citadel (1978–1982), and East Carolina (1985–1988). After compiling an overall career record of 302-176-6, Baker served as a key administrator at USC. He is a member of both the Sumter and Fellowship of Christian Athletes Halls of Fame. (Citadel Military College.)

WEEMS BASKIN, 1973. The popular, cigar-chomping, longtime USC track coach (1948–1969) with a 90-47 dual meet record was named a member of the National Track and Field Hall of Fame for his feats as the national and international high hurdles champion in 1928. As an Auburn athlete, he once held the world High Hurdles record and won three Southern Conference championships. He is also a member of the State of Georgia, and Helms Athletic Foundations Halls of Fame. He served as a key contributor to the SCAHOF board. (University of South Carolina.)

MARVIN BASS, 1992. Pictured on the right, the USC football coach (1961–1965) went on to become a Canadian Football League head coach and an NFL assistant coach. Although he compiled a 17-29-4 record, he built he the team into ACC champions in 1965; however, the conference vacated the title because of two ineligible players. The former All-Southern Conference star at William and Mary is also a member of the Virginia Sports Hall of Fame. (Safran Antiques.)

CHARLES F. BOLDEN, 1982. A standout athlete at Columbia's Booker T. Washington High School and Johnson C. Smith University, Bolden later served as football coach and athletic director at C. A. Johnson and Keenan High Schools and compiled 150-plus victories. He also served as SCAHOF executive secretary. Richland County named a football stadium in Bolden's honor in 1980. His son Charles F. Bolden Jr. became an astronaut and in 2009 was named the head of NASA. (Bolden family.)

JIM CARLEN, 2006. A football coach with a career coaching record of 45-36-1 at USC; Carlen's 8-4 Gator Bowl team of 1980 ended up ranked 15th in the nation. Before joining the Gamecocks, Carlen had coached successfully at West Virginia and Texas Tech. (University of South Carolina.)

OLIVER DAWSON, 1974. South Carolina State named its football stadium after its longtime football coach (1937–1950). Dawson also coached tennis, track, and golf. The Cleveland native starred at John Carroll University in football, basketball, baseball, tennis, and boxing. (South Carolina State University.)

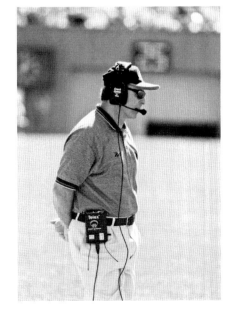

FISHER DEBERRY, 2002. The Cheraw native and two-sport star at Wofford went on to become the winningest Air Force Academy football coach of all time, building a record of 169-109-1 over 23 years, during which he guided the Falcons to 12 bowl games. He earned the Kodak National Coach of Year award in 1985. (Air Force Academy.)

RAY "RED" DOBSON, 1977. The 1920s Furman football, basketball, baseball and swimming star later won five football championships and six basketball titles as a coach at Spartanburg High School. (Furman University.)

REX ENRIGHT, 1960. The beloved longtime USC football coach (1938–1942 and 1946–1955) and athletic director (1938–1960) coached the team to a 64-69-7 record. He played fullback at Notre Dame and two years with the Green Bay Packers. USC named its athletic offices after the Rockford, Illinois, native. Enright is a charter member of the South Carolina Athletic Hall of Fame. (University of South Carolina.)

DANNY FORD, 1982. The 1981 National Coach of the Year led Clemson to a national championship at age 33. Over the years, Ford compiled a 96-29-4 record with the Tigers and won five ACC titles. His teams won six of the eight bowl games in which they played, and from 1981 to 1983, his combined record of 30-2-2 was best among all college coaches. While at Clemson, the Gadsden, Alabama, native coached 71 first-team All-ACC stars and 26 All-Americans; eleven of his players went on to win Super Bowl rings. (Clemson University.)

CALLY GAULT, 1988. The Bamberg native and three-sports star at Presbyterian College (1944–1948) later turned to coaching at North Augusta High School (88-13-7 record including 42 straight victories) and then at Presbyterian College (127-101-6 from 1962 to 1984), where he earned five South Carolina Coach of the Year awards. (Presbyterian College.)

BOBBY GILES, 2009. Olympia High School's longtime coach compiled an overall 623-281-4 record and won seven state championships in three sports. In football he recorded a 110-87-4 mark with one title; in basketball, he compiled a 336-116 record with five titles; in baseball, he had a 207-78 record and one state crown. Giles served as Shrine Bowl coach in 1967, and coached two players (Jerry Martin and Mike Martin) who went on to play major league baseball. As an athlete, Giles played football and basketball at USC. He scored the first TD in Gator Bowl history, and his 60-yard quick kick held the Gator Bowl distance record for 23 years. (Giles family.)

GEORGE GLYMPH, 1999. Columbia native Glymph coached Eau Claire High School to five South Carolina basketball championships and recorded a 471-135 mark from 1974–1996 before moving on to assistant coaching jobs in the NBA with Portland, Indiana, and New York. Glymph served as a father figure to a host of Eau Claire players, including future NBA star Jermaine O'Neal. Eau Claire High School named its gymnasium in his honor. (Glymph family.)

NEILD GORDON, 1978. Furman basketball star became NAIA National Coach of Year in 1977 for coaching Newberry to a 36-1 record. He later started Winthrop's basketball program. (Furman University.)

MAX GRUBBS, 1981. The Anderson College tennis coach and athletics director (1958–1977) mentored both the men's and women's teams. He also coached the basketball, baseball, and track teams. His tennis teams experienced only one losing season in 20 years. (Anderson College.)

SYLVIA HATCHELL, 2009. Hatchell compiled a 272-80 coaching record over 11 seasons and won two national championships at Francis Marion. She continued her success with the NCAA crown at the University of North Carolina in 1994 and entered the 2009–2010 season with a 538-202 UNC record for an overall mark of 810-282. Hatchell is the only coach to win titles in all three NCAA divisions. The two-time National Coach of the Year (1999 and 2006) is a member of the Women's Basketball Hall of Fame and North Carolina Sports Hall of Fame. She led the USA team to a gold medal in the 1995 World University Games, and has served as an assistant on five USA gold medal teams. (University of North Carolina.)

JOHN W. HEISMAN, 1978. College football's most prestigious trophy is named for this coaching innovator. Heisman coached at Clemson from 1900 to 1903, recording a 19-3-1 mark–still the best winning percentage in school history–and took the Tigers to their first bowl, an 11-11 tie against Cumberland in 1903. Heisman also coached the Clemson baseball team (1901–1903) with a 28-6-1 record for a school-best .814 winning percentage. Heisman, who invented such football basics as the center snap and handoff, also introduced such trick plays as the double-lateral, flea-flicker, and hidden-ball, and pioneered the forward pass. His career lasted 36 years, beginning in 1892 at Oberlin University and continuing at seven colleges including Clemson University. He compiled a career record of 185-70-17. (Clemson University.)

FRANK HOWARD, 1961. The legendary Clemson football coach and one of sport's all-time colorful characters compiled a 165-118-12 record from 1940 to 1969). His teams won six ACC titles and Howard is a member of five halls of fame. Clemson commemorates his memory at every home football game when the team rubs "Howard's Rock" before running down the "Death Valley" hill onto the field. The "Baron of Barlow Bend" (Alabama) is buried in the cemetery on the hill above Memorial Stadium. (Clemson University.)

COACHING CHAMPIONS

I. M. IBRAHIM, 2007. Ibrahim coached Clemson to 17 NCAA tournaments, 11 ACC titles, 19 Top 20 national rankings, and national soccer championships in 1984 and 1987. The native of Haifa, Israel, recorded a 388-102-31 mark and his success helped popularize soccer in the state of South Carolina and in the South. (Clemson University.)

WILLIE JEFFRIES, 1996. The Union native coached at Lancaster Barr Street High School (1960) and Gaffney Graward High School (1964–1968) with a combined 65-7-2 record and three state championships. He went on to become the beloved South Carolina State University coach (90-38-4 over 12 years in two stints: 1973–1978 and 1989–1994). He became the first black head football coach in NCAA Division I when named to coach Wichita State University in 1979. Jeffries' teams produced a host of NFL stars. After retiring, Jeffries became a SCAHOF board president and banquet emcee. (South Carolina State University.)

WALTER JOHNSON, 1960. The longtime Presbyterian football coach and athletic director (from 1915 to his death in 1958) is a charter member of the South Carolina Athletic Hall of Fame. The "genial Swede" fought in World War II and compiled a 183-96-19 coaching record. (Presbyterian College.)

WHITIE KENDALL, 1986. The longtime Greenville-Parker High School coach won 11 state championships–five in basketball, three in football, and three in baseball.

HARVEY KIRKLAND, 1993. Before the arrival of John McKissick, this Batesburg native coached Summerville High School to a 72-18-7 record, including state championships in 1948 and 1949. The onetime Newberry College football and baseball star (1934–1937) then coached his alma mater in football (1952–1968), compiling a lifetime 72-77-11 mark, including two bowl game appearances. He twice won South Carolina Coach of the Year honors (1953, 1962) and is a member of the Carolinas Conference Hall of Fame. (Newberry College.)

JOHN KRESSE, 2001. The dynamic College of Charleston coach had a 23-year career with a 560-143 record; his .797 winning percentage ranked second among active college coaches when he retired. He averaged 24 victories a year and led Cougars to the 1983 NAIA National Championship and four Southern Conference titles. (College of Charleston.)

BILLY LAVAL, 1961. From the 1920s to the 1950s, Laval coached at Furman (winning seven state championships), USC, Emory and Henry, and Newberry College, with a cumulative 94-76 career record. At various times he coached football, baseball, and basketball. (Safran Antiques.)

CATHERINE LEMPESIS, 2007. A star runner (finishing eighth in the Boston Marathon Masters Division, and at one time ranked the seventh best female marathoner in the world, Lempesis became a star running coach, leading Columbia-area teams to 15 state titles and 6 runner-up spots, beginning in 1986. The Road Runners Hall of Famer and South Carolina Track and Field Hall of Famer also led efforts for gender equity for South Carolina female coaches. (Lempesis family.)

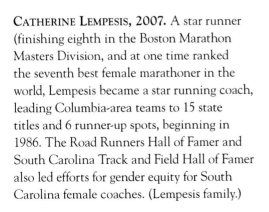

FRANK McGUIRE, 1973. The legendary USC basketball coach was enshrined in the Basketball Hall of Fame in 1997. He won National Coach of the Year three times with three different colleges (St. John's, University of North Carolina, and University of South Carolina), won the NCAA championship at the University of North Carolina in 1957, and finished his 30-year career with a record of 550-235, including 283-142 with the Gamecocks from 1964 to 1980. (University of South Carolina.)

JOHN McKISSICK, 1982. Summerville High School's coaching legend ranks as the winningest football coach in history at any level—high school, college, or professional. His teams have won 10 state championships while compiling a 565-133-13 record from 1952 to the start of the 2009 season, making him the nation's longest serving active coach. The three-time coach of the year is a member of the National High School Sports Hall of Fame. McKissick's coaching career started from humble beginnings: after accepting his first coaching job via telephone to tiny Clarkton High School in North Carolina, McKissick found out when he arrived that he had inherited a six-man football team. Unsure of how to proceed, McKissick called his former coach, Lonnie McMillian at Presbyterian College, to say he didn't know anything about six-man football. "Son," said McMillian, "you don't know anything about eleven-man football, either. Just do your homework and work as hard as you can, and act like you know exactly what you're doing." (Summerville High School.)

DUTCH McLEAN, 1962. As a member of Newberry College's first football team in the early 1900s, McLean scored 17 touchdowns in a 139-0 victory over Baylor Academy. He captained the football and basketball teams as a player, and went on to coach Newberry's teams from 1921 to 1937, with a 43-96-11 record. (Newberry College.)

LONNIE McMILLIAN, 1974. Serving Presbyterian College (1923–1959) as its longtime football coach, McMillian, from Prescott, Arkansas, also coached three other sports at various times. As a Presbyterian College athlete, McMillian made All-State in 1919 and 1920. He is credited with giving Clemson its stadium nickname. After Presbyterian College lost at Clemson in the mid-1940s, McMillian called Memorial Stadium "Death Valley," because his teams went there to die. The name stuck. (Presbyterian College.)

JAMES "SLICK" MOORE, 1987. The Greenville High School three-sport star of the late 1920s became the school's basketball coach and led his teams to seven state championships while compiling a 254-58 record. He also coached Greenville to two state golf titles, and the 1962 state football crown. Greenville High School named its gym in his honor. (Moore family.)

JAMES MOORER, 1975. The Sims High School three-sport coaching great guided his football teams to a 135-3-5 record. His team once won 69 straight games. (Sims High School.)

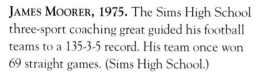

JOE MORRISON, 1989. The versatile 14-year NFL standout played seven positions with the New York Giants, who retired his jersey. As USC's football coach, the Lima, Ohio, native compiled a 39-28-2 record and took the Gamecocks to two bowl games between 1983 and 1988, including a 10-2 record in the Black Magic season of 1984. (University of South Carolina.)

WILLIAM "RED" MYERS, 1992. The three-sports star at Erskine College (1947–1950) went on to become an outstanding basketball coach at Dreher High School and then on to his alma mater college, where he coached his teams to an overall 413-292 record (1958–1982). He was elected to the NAIA Hall Of Fame in 1981. In 2009, Erskine named its basketball in his honor. Before he began coaching basketball, Myers's Dreher High School teams won two state championships in football and two in track. (Erskine College.)

JESS NEELY, 1981. A star player at Vanderbilt before becoming Clemson's head coach (1931–1939), Neely the Tigers to their first bowl—the 1940 Cotton Bowl—and compiled an overall 43-35-7 record. Then he moved to Rice University, where his teams won four Southwest Conference titles. He is a member of the College Football Hall of Fame. (Clemson University.)

RICK "ROCK" NORMAN, 1968. The longtime basketball, football and track coach at Furman (1923-28), USC (1928–1936), and the Citadel (1936–1939) finally ended his career at Clemson (1940–1957), where his track teams won seven state titles. He compiled an overall career record of 125-114, and received the ACC's Service to Sports Award for "long, distinguished and unselfish service to athletics." Clemson named its outdoor track complex in his honor. (Clemson University.)

MOONEY PLAYER, 1998. A colorful character and master motivator, Player coached five high school state football championship teams (1962 and 1963 at Saluda High School, and 1965, 1967, and 1970 at Lower Richland High School). A lover of surprise plays, he compiled a lifetime 157-22-7 record for an amazing .877 winning percentage. (Player family.)

CHAL PORT, 1994. The longtime baseball coach at the Citadel compiled a 641-386-2 record over 27 years (1965–1991) and won three Southern Conference titles. He was named National Coach of Year in 1990 when he led Bulldogs to fifth place in the College World Series. The former University of North Carolina pitching star also served on the NCAA selection committee. (Citadel.)

H. B. "BEE" RHAME, 1979.
The early-1920s USC baseball
and football standout became
a premier football, baseball,
and track coach at Columbia
High School. Over 23 years of
coaching football, his teams
compiled a 191-34-13 record.
The Holly Hill native coached
teams to eight state titles in
basketball, three in baseball,
and five in track before retiring
in 1950. (Rhame family.)

**J. HERBERT ROLLINS,
1983.** The four-sport
star at Lake City and
Presbyterian College
compiled a 611-180
high school coaching
record at Olanta High
School, Kingstree
High School, and Lake
City High School.
(Rollins family.)

PAUL SCARPA, 2010. Still active, Scarpa had by 2009 already recorded a 729-448 record in 43 years, including 37 years at Furman, where his tennis teams earned a 216-32 mark and 14 Southern Conference titles, and Scarpa himself won seven Coach of the Year awards. Scarpa ranks first among active coaches in career victories. The NCAA adopted the Scarpa System for dual-match scoring rules; he also invented and patented the Tenex tape used to mark clay courts around the world. The Charleston native starred as a player at Florida State University. He is a member of the South Carolina Tennis Hall of Fame, and the Furman University courts bear his name. (Furman University.)

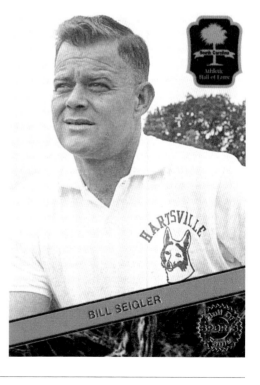

BILL SEIGLER, 1984. After starring in football and baseball at Newberry College, Seigler became a successful high school coach, mostly at Hartsville and Hanahan High Schools. The two-time coach of the year (1958, 1965) compiled a 192-34-5 record over 22 years (1950–1972). (Hartsville High School.)

DICK SHERIDAN, 2004. The North Augusta native's Furman football teams dominated the Southern Conference from 1978–1985, when Sheridan coached the Paladins to eight league championships with an overall 69-23-1 record. He was named National 1-AA Coach of Year in 1985 before moving to North Carolina State and coaching his teams there to an overall 52-29-1 mark. (North Carolina State University.)

JOHN J. "CY" SZAKACSI, 1996. Known as the "Happy Hungarian," Szakasci arrived from Ohio to attend the University of South Carolina on the GI Bill after World War II. After starring for the Gamecocks' baseball and basketball teams, Szakasci remained in the Palmetto State to compile a 34-year, 605-226 high school basketball coaching mark at three schools from 1959 to 1986, winning five state crowns, and a National Coach of Year Award. In addition to basketball, Szakasci coached title teams in three other sports. (Szakacsi family.)

JIM TATUM, 1975. The McColl native compiled a 100-34-7 record as football coach at Maryland State University, Oklahoma State University, and the University of North Carolina. His Maryland team won the national championship in 1953, and Tatum was named NCAA Coach of the Year. (South Carolina Athletic Hall of Fame.)

J. C. "JAKIE" TODD, 1962. The diminutive "Little Colonel" served as Erskine's football, basketball, and baseball coach from 1926 to 1941. As a football star, he and Dode Phillips led the Flying Fleet to upset football victories over USC in 1917 and Clemson in 1921. (Erskine College.)

ANNIE TRIBBLE, 1994. The pioneer women's basketball coach's Anderson College teams won three junior college national titles and enjoyed seven 20-win seasons, compiling a 355-168 record. Tribble then moved on to Clemson University, where her teams compiled a 200-135 mark at from 1976 to 1987. In 1980-1981, she led Clemson to the 1980–1981 regular-season ACC title. She is a charter member of the U.S. Women's Basketball Association. (Clemson University.)

COACHING CHAMPIONS

WILLIE VARNER, 1985. The Woodruff coach's teams won 10 state football championships and recorded a 382-126-10 mark over 43 years (second in Palmetto State history), beginning in 1954. He also coached four girls' basketball state titles and two baseball crowns. The 1983 National Coach of the Year is a member of the National Coaches Hall of Fame. (Woodruff High School.)

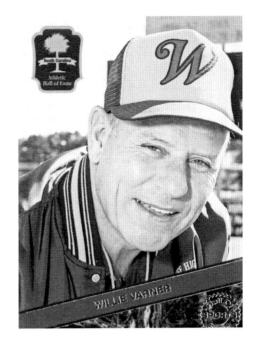

DONNIE WALSH, 2006. Coach Frank McGuire's top assistant in USC's glory years of 1970s, Walsh went on to become one of NBA's most respected front office administrators and talent evaluators as the general manager of the Indiana Pacers and New York Knicks. (Indian Pacers.)

TAFT WATSON, 1994. The legendary Terrell's Bay High School basketball coach arrived in 1949 and his teams went on to win eight state championships over the ensuing decades; in 1994, he coached both the boys and girls to Class A state titles. His boys' teams compiled an overall 742-313 record. (Watson family.)

SHANNON WILKERSON, 1977. The Marion High School basketball coach from 1942 through 1966, Wilkerson and her teams compiled a 437-32-5 record, which at one point included 105 straight victories. In the process, the team won seven state championships. (Safran Antiques.)

CARL WILLIAMS, 2008. The only coach to lead three different high schools to state championships (Booker T. Washington in 1970, Flora in 1981 and 1986, and Lower Richland in 1999), Williams' teams won 503 games overall. Three of his players went on to play in the NBA. (Williams family.)

SAM WYCHE, 1994. A star quarterback at Furman (1963–1965), Wyche played in the NFL and later became a head coach. The Atlanta native was named 1988 NFL Coach of Year after he took his 12-4 Bengals to the Super Bowl. Additionally, Wyche is credited as the innovator of the no-huddle offense. (Furman University.)

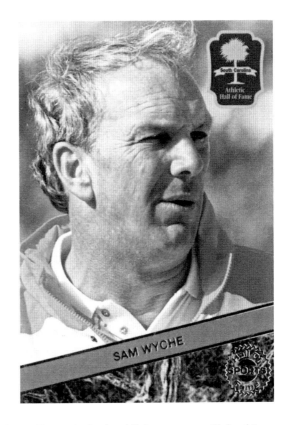

STAN ZUK, 1978. An All-American at Columbia University in 1933, and later a fullback for the New York Giants, Zuk, working as an unpaid volunteer, served as football coach and father figure to the Epworth Orphanage team from 1946 to 1952. His squads compiled a 53-5-3 record against area high schools while playing with an average squad roster of just 14 players, all wearing hand-me-down, altered uniforms from USC. Zuk's best team, the undefeated 1951 "Runts," averaged 147 pounds on the front line. The school became so dominant that high school teams began refusing to play the Eagles, and Epworth Orphanage had to drop the sport. The Buffalo, New York, native won several World War II medals (Army Commendation, Asiatic Pacific, American Defense, American Campaign, Armed Forces Reserve, and two overseas bars). He retired as a major and served a director of the Veterans Administration Regional Office in Columbia until he retired in 1973. (South Carolina Athletic Hall of Fame.)

Not Pictured

A. P. "Dizzy" McLeod, 1968. The former Furman athlete returned as a coach and guided Paladins' basketball teams to a 69-17 record from 1928 to 1931, giving McLeod the best winning percentage of any Furman hoops coach to date. In 1932, he took over the Furman football team and they compiled a 59-7-5 record over 11 seasons.

Cliff Morgan, 1990. A three-sport athlete at Newberry College (1934–1937) and then a three-sport coach at Summerville, Marion, and Orangeburg High Schools, Morgan also played semiprofessional baseball and served in World War II.

6

CONSCIENTIOUS
CONTRIBUTORS

You don't have to be a fantastic hero to do certain things—to compete.
You can just be an ordinary chap, sufficiently motivated to reach challenging goals.

—Sir Edmund Hillary

The South Carolina Athletic Hall of Fame, like most national and state sports shrines, realizes there should be a place of honor for non-athletes who contribute, in some special way, to the betterment of sports. To that end, SCAHOF has enshrined a handful of behind-the-scenes types who aided the cause of sports in the Palmetto State.

Bickering among USC and Clemson supporters rivals that of political parties on Capitol Hill. But among the battling of the athletes and bitterness of the state's two major colleges, Bob Bradley and Tom Price maintained a genuine friendship. "Mr. B." always had a smile and a joke for the media, and "T. P." never let a statistic escape his grasp. Both sports information directors served as buffers when criticism managed to rile coaches and fans of the Tigers and Gamecocks.

Herman Helms, who came from the *Charlotte Observer* to the *State* in Columbia in the early 1960s and spearheaded the revival of the then dormant South Carolina Athletic Hall of Fame, stood foremost among the Palmetto State's press. Although he exercised the power of the pen, he also applauded the spirit of sports—especially football and boxing.

Bob Fulton, outlasted many a football and basketball coach and athletic director at USC as its longtime broadcaster, often entertained post-game press gatherings with his good humor and tales that could not be recounted in print or over the airwaves.

Others made unchartered inroads into sports. Cot Campbell bounced around in a variety of odd jobs, including circus-type barking at a Florida animal park, before founding an Atlanta advertising agency and chucking it all to introduce America to shared ownership in racehorses in 1969.

Unlike Campbell's risky venture, the late Mrs. Marion duPont Scott had plenty of funding—her own family fortune—to start the first $100,000 steeplechase in the nation: the Colonial Cup in Camden. She spared no efforts to establish the race, paying all travel expenses for each horse, groom, trainer, and owner from several countries to compete with the best jumpers in America. Her generosity works on behalf of the people of Camden every day; proceeds from the two annual Camden races benefit the Kershaw County hospital. Likewise, Bob McNair's business fortunes have allowed him to enter sports ownership and become overwhelmingly philanthropic.

A case can be made that Bob Colvin and Harold Brasington played a key role in the building of the NASCAR empire. Colvin labored diligently to promote Darlington. In 1962 one superstitious driver refused to come for the 13th annual Southern 500, so the persuasive Colvin billed the event as "the 12th renewal" of the race. The driver entered the race field.

BOB BRADLEY AND TOM PRICE, 2008. Bradley, Clemson's beloved publicity man, served as the school's unofficial ambassador from 1955–1989. The Tigers named their press box in his honor. He also served as the ACC Tournament's official scorer for many years and as a SCAHOF board member. (SCAHOF inductee 2001) Longtime, award-winning Tom Price served USC from 1962 to 2008 and authored several Gamecock sports books. It is said that the two men never let their schools' often-frenzied rivalry stand in the way of their friendship. (Clemson University.)

BOB FULTON, 1990. A broadcaster for 53 years and radio's "Voice of the Gamecocks" for 43 years, Fulton was named eight times as South Carolina Sportscaster of the Year. He outlasted nine Carolina football coaches, ten basketball coaches, and nine athletics directors. During his career, the USC Hall of Famer also did national radio for major league baseball games over the Mutual Broadcasting Network, and worked play-by-play for six Bluebonnet Bowls, two Gator Bowls, and a Sun Bowl. (University of South Carolina.)

COT CAMPBELL, 2007. Campbell pioneered Thoroughbred ownership in 1969 as founder-president of the Aiken-based Dogwood Stables, a perennial top ten outfit, which included Summer Squall, the 1990 Preakness winner and Kentucky Derby runner-up. Under Campbell's guidance, Dogwood has produced two Eclipse Award champions, six millionaires, and more than 70 stakes winners. (Dogwood Stable.)

HERMAN HELMS, 2009. The principled sports editor and award-winning columnist for the *State* newspaper stood for diverse coverage and, as a sports columnist, served as the conscience of USC and Clemson athletics. He also revived a dormant South Carolina Athletic Hall of Fame in the 1960s and served as its longtime director. He is also a member of the Carolina Boxing Hall of Fame and the Catawba College Hall of Fame. (Helms family.)

HAROLD BRASINGTON, 2002. The former dirt track stock car racer was running a construction company when he had the vision of turning a patch of land into NASCAR's Darlington International Raceway. "Harold's Folly" was the host of the world's first 500-mile race in 1950. (Brasington family.)

BOB MCNAIR, 2010. This University of South Carolina graduate owns the NFL Houston Texans and a successful stable of Thoroughbred racehorses based in Aiken. He and his wife, Janice (who herself hails from the Orangeburg area and attended Columbia College), have donated millions to their alma maters and other charities. He is a member of the Texas Business Hall of Fame. (Houston Texans.)

MARION DUPONT SCOTT, 2003. The Grand Lady of Steeplechasing saved the popular Carolina Cup race from extinction and started the Colonial Cup in Camden in 1971 as America's first $100,000 horse race over jumps. In her will, she left her 500-acre Springdale Race Course to the state of South Carolina. (National Steeplechasing Museum.)

BOB COLVIN, 1977. Cofounder with Harold Brasington of the Darlington International Raceway, Colvin served as the longtime president of NASCAR. He labored diligently to make Darlington the sport's showcase. For example, in 1962 one top—and very superstitious—driver did not want to race in the 13th annual Southern 500, so Colvin changed the billing to the "12th Renewal" of the race. The driver entered the race field.

INDEX

An asterisk indicates that the hall of famer is deceased.

DISCOVER THOUSANDS OF LOCAL HISTORY BOOKS FEATURING MILLIONS OF VINTAGE IMAGES

Arcadia Publishing, the leading local history publisher in the United States, is committed to making history accessible and meaningful through publishing books that celebrate and preserve the heritage of America's people and places.

Find more books like this at
www.arcadiapublishing.com

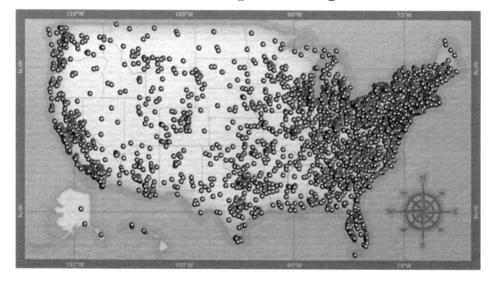

Search for your hometown history, your old stomping grounds, and even your favorite sports team.